Poland from the Inside

Poland from the Inside

Bertram de Colonna

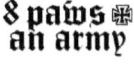

The Scriptorium

First published in 1939: Bertram de Colonna, *Poland from the Inside,* Heath Cranton Limited, London.

Reprint ©2022 by The Scriptorium.
wintersonnenwende.com
versandbuchhandelscriptorium.com

A Note to the Reader: please pardon the occasional wrong hyphenation at the end of lines. The software with which this book is printed inserts these hyphens automatically, and manual corrections of errors are almost impossible.

Our cover design is based on the flag of Poland adopted in 1919, and on an outline map of Europe, 1929-1938, courtesy of Wikipedia.

Print edition ISBN 978-1-7781445-4-7
ebook ISBN 978-1-7781445-5-4

All rights reserved. No part of this book may be reproduced in any manner whatsoever without written permission except in the case of brief quotations embodied in critical articles and reviews.

CONTENTS

	Introduction	1
1	Historical Survey	3
2	Economic Life	8
3	Composition of Population	14
4	The Constitution	20
5	The problem of Danzig	23
6	On tour in Poland	42
7	A Nationality State	49
8	Dreams of Empire	56
9	The Poles at home	65
10	The influence of Napoleon	70
11	Famous men quoted	78
12	The small nationalities	85

CONTENTS

13 | Treatment of minorities 94

14 | Upper Silesia's example 99

15 | Conclusions 105

16 | Facsimile Appendix 113

Introduction

Poland is a country which, in its present form, was founded after the Great War. In order to obtain some idea of its size, one must remember that it is almost three times as large as England.

Poland is bounded on the North by Latvia, Lithuania, East Prussia, Danzig and the Baltic, on the East by Russia, and on the West by Germany, while in the South it borders Rumania, Slovakia and Hungary. The part extending to the Baltic forms a wedge between East Prussia and the rest of Germany, and is generally referred to as the Corridor.

The country comprises a part of White Russia, a part of the Ukraine, Upper Silesia, which voted in favour of a union with Germany after the Great War, and, in addition to the Corridor, several mainly non-Polish territories, while the originally Polish kernel is in the centre of the present State.

The Vistula is the main river, but its commercial importance has been reduced considerably since the War, and it is, as Polish figures show, not the main commercial highway. Poland's seaport, Gdynia, shares with Danzig the main part of overseas commerce. Gdynia has been extended of recent years.

Danzig is not part of Poland, but is called a Free State. It has its own officials, its own postage stamps, its own currency and its own laws; but it forms with Poland a customs union, so that Poland was permitted by the terms of the peace treaty to post her customs officials there.

In former centuries, under the Polish kings, the country played an important part in European history every now and then. Later on, it was divided between the neighbouring States, Russia obtaining the lion's share. There were three partitions altogether.

The Poles wished to regain their independence and struggled against the Russians. During the Great War their opportunity came, and as early as 1916 Germany promised the representatives of the Poles independence.

When the frontiers of the new Poland were fixed, vast tracts of non-Polish land were included, and there were loud protests in England when Upper Silesia was added as well. In the course of time, however, this was forgotten, and most people now believe that the provinces making up the Polish Republic have always been Polish.

The Poles are of Slavonic origin, but absolutely distinct from the Russians.

Their main occupation is agriculture, but there are also important manufacturing centres, especially in the former German part in the South-West. The people are almost all Roman Catholics.

Geographically and historically, the whole country now composing Poland belongs to no single, compact State system, but comprises a number of various sections synthetically linked up under the rule of Warsaw. Ethnographically, the South is Ukrainian, much of the West German, the extreme North also German, part of the North-East Russian, while the rest of the Republic is mainly Polish, but with no inconsiderable admixture of other nationalities. The present frontiers were mainly due to Polish claims to have owned these areas in earlier centuries.

1

Historical Survey

Poland's claim to be a great realm is based upon what is said to be history. The Poles state that their country once stretched to the very centre of Europe. But the truth is that the Slavonic groups distributed thinly throughout this area were by no means all Polish. The mere fact that a few families settled for a while in this or that district does not offer a good basis for a legal claim on the part of a State.

Historically, Poland first made her mark in the 10th century, when she was a kind of vassal State linked up with the German Empire. The first actual reference to the State as such was in the year 963. Shortly afterwards, Poland became the centre of wholesale fighting between Slavonic tribes. This was really the beginning of the struggles between the Russians and the Poles, which did not end when the Czarist regime fell, but continued until the Poles drove the Bolsheviks across the frontiers at a time when peace was supposed to have succeeded the Great War.

Internal dissention was fairly general under Mieczyslav II and III, Casimir I and II, Boleslav II, III, IV and V, and the three Vladislavs, as well as under Leszek the White, Leszek the Black and Przemyslav. The latter was murdered. But during their rule the sovereignty of the German Empire was repeatedly acknowledged. All these Polish rulers bore the title of Duke, and it was not until the 14th century that a king was crowned and a certain amount of law and order established, in place of the struggles between the rival ducal factions. Shortly after, Poland was united with Hungary, but this was purely a personal union under King Louis (1370-1382), which ceased on his death.

Peace was not, however, to last long. The nobles repeatedly tried to overawe the people, and there was later a war with Sweden. In the second half of the seventeenth century civil war broke out.

Domestic strife actually survived two partitions, the second in 1793, when most of the formerly Polish territory went to Russia, with a population of 3 millions, while Prussia received a strip with 1,100,000 inhabitants. Kosciusco tried in 1794 to unite the Poles, and many poems tell of his prowess. But shortly afterwards he was defeated at Praga (not to be confused with Prague in Bohemia), and a third partition took place, Russia, Prussia and Austria obtaining the territory. Russia again took over the largest part. During the Napoleonic wars, the Poles established a kind of independence, following the Peace of Tilsit. The Peace of Vienna added to this Polish State, and hopes were placed in Napoleon by many Poles. But they were doomed to disappointment. All the French wished for in Poland was to raise an army to help the "petit caporal" defeat Russia. In 1812 the new State, known as the Duchy of Warsaw, came to a sudden collapse. In 1815 the Poles were promised a certain representation, with two chambers, by Czar Alexander I. The first Parliament did meet, it is true, but it had no real power, and things became still worse when Alexander died. In 1830 the Poles revolted, and drove the Russians across the borders. The Polish nobility took over the reins of government, but party strife prevented any real work of reconstruction. The nobles and people could not agree, and the way was thus paved for the return of the Russians. Chlopicki established himself as dictator, and tried to negotiate with Russia, with the object of keeping the Polish people from overruling the nobility, but the Russians demanded complete capitulation. Had the Poles remained united, they could have maintained their full independence, but when one party endeavoured to make terms with Russia at the expense of the other, Poland lost her liberty. Marshal Diebitsch assembled an army of 120,000 men, and advanced on Warsaw. After brave resistance, the Poles were defeated, and their leader sought refuge in Austria. It is interesting to note that in 1831, just over a century ago, the Poles appealed for aid in London and Paris, but met with little sympathy.

Most of those known to have played a leading part in the revolt were sent to Siberia in chains, a few escaped to Austria and Prussia. The frontiers were occupied by secret police, and Poland was to all intents and purposes cut off from all connection with foreign States. For long years no Pole could attend a university, while in 1833 a law demanded that only Russian schools could be attended. In 1840 an edict declared that no person without a perfect command of the Russian language might occupy a public position.

News circulated slowly in those days, but the world was aware of these happenings. No single State offered to assist the Poles. Polish revolutionaries gathered in Germany, France and Italy, as well as, on a smaller scale, in England. The Poles under Prussia also attempted a rising, but their leaders were imprisoned. In contrast to Russia, Berlin pardoned the revolutionaries after a brief period of imprisonment, and promised the Poles a settlement in accordance with their wishes on condition that they refrained from further risings while the arrangements were being made. The Poles continued to arm, however, although their own schools, courts and administrative bodies were speedily established, and a Prussian force was dispatched to end the revolt.

One insurrection followed the other in Russian Poland. In 1867 the Czar even went so far as to refuse the Polish clergy all contact with Rome, and the property of Poles was confiscated. There was little improvement when the present century dawned, and a bitter hatred of the Russians prevails in Poland to this day, for after the Bolshevik revolution the new Moscow authorities showed no change of attitude.

The Poles and Germans lived in parts of Prussia on fairly good terms in more recent years preceding the War. Conditions improved as a result of Germany's industrial expansion, which assured ample opportunities for all. Many Poles were more than satisfied, and when the Great War came they fought solidly with the Germans and Austrians, while those compelled to serve with the Russian army deserted at the first opportunity. There were, however, exceptions, and some Poles dreamed of an Empire stretching to Berlin and Stettin. Indeed, one side of the River Havel, which almost skirts Berlin, was repeatedly quoted as Polish. The War did not fulfil their dreams. It brought them areas containing many non-Poles, but not the vast Empire they had hoped for. Lithuania was also to be included and, as a matter of fact, the Vilna district was taken from the Lithuanians by the Poles in defiance to the Allies. The most recent addition to the Polish Republic is Teschen, which was Warsaw's share in the partition of Czecho-Slovakia. Its cession to Poland resulted in new dreams of Empire.

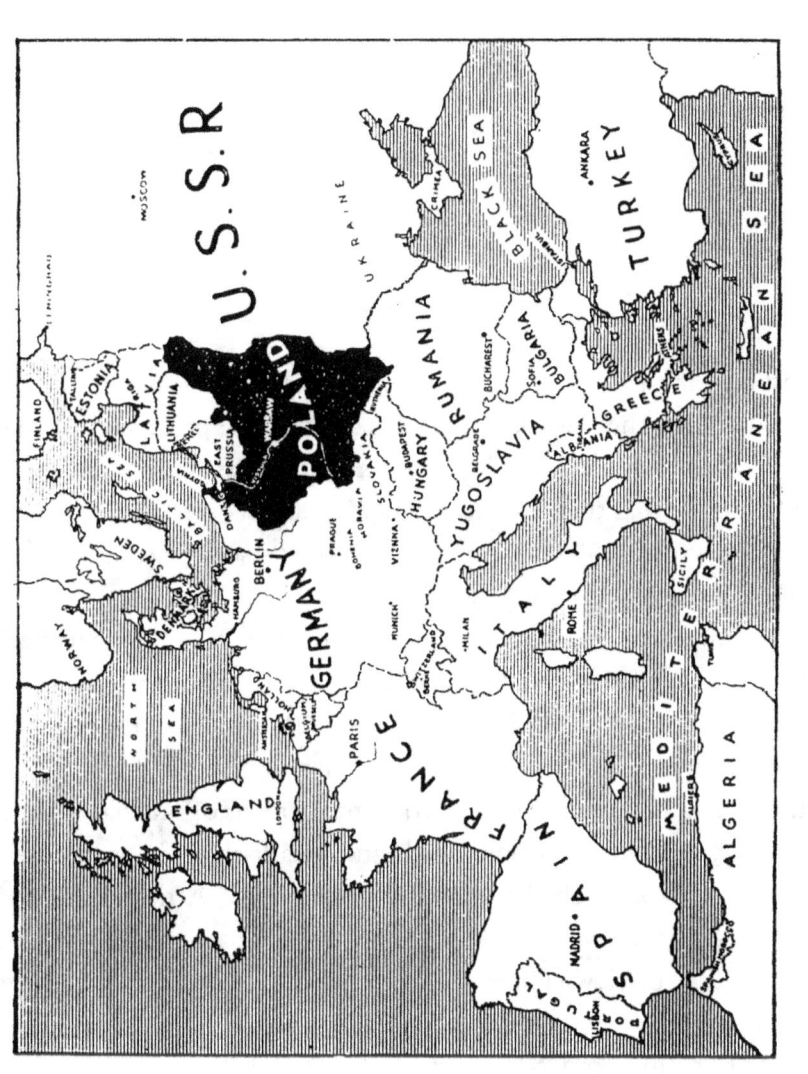

Map showing the position of Poland.

2

Economic Life

Most people have an entirely incorrect idea of the economic structure of Poland. When the possibilities of this country are being considered, the area and the population are quoted as proof of its latent purchasing power. It is true that there are nearly 35,000,000 people in Poland, and that the area is over 150,000 square miles, but these facts cannot alone serve as evidence of its latent possibilities.

A decisive factor for the economic structure of Poland is that there are considerable economic differences between its various parts. These differences are noticeable in all fields. The new Poland is not the result of a process of evolution, but was pieced together after the Great War. The various parts were included in the economic systems of Russia, Austria or Germany, and had their own needs and peculiarities, in accordance with the States to which they previously belonged. A new State was established, but there was a lack of co-ordination, particularly from an economic point of view. There was also a great difference in the life of the people in the several parts.

Big contrasts in population conditions are to be observed in the areas of Posen, the Corridor and Upper Silesia (formerly Prussian) as well as Galicia (formerly Austrian), on the one hand, and the ten gouvernements of Czarist Russia, while the contrast with Vilna and Novogrodek is equally great. In the North-East, the White Russians form a solid majority, while in the South the Ukrainians make up the major part of the population. The Jews form a big percentage of the citizens of the big towns of former Russian sections, while in the district of the Vistula and Warta, solid settlements of Germans are met with.

The biggest group, which incidentally has the greatest relative density, is in Galicia, with 8,500,000 inhabitants, and a density of population quoted by Polish books of reference as varying between 110 and 132 per square kilometre. As, however, the thinly populated mountain districts are included, the actual density in the area round Cracow and Lemberg is much greater. The southern parts of the former Russian Poland have also a big surplus population.

On the other hand, the formerly German provinces of Posen and the Corridor have a population density of only 80 and 66 per square kilometre, and in purely agricultural areas a density of 40 is not uncommon. The growth of the population is, again, most marked in the parts already overpopulated, while the surplus rural population in Galicia, in the southern part of Russian Poland and in East Poland threatens to become a real danger.

For example, Polish figures show that the number of persons engaged in agricultural pursuits per 100 [h]ectares (nearly 250 acres) of arable land is up to 150 in Galicia, but only 40 to 50 in Posen and the Corridor. Conditions in the rural parts of Galicia, as well as in some parts of East Poland and sectors of the former Russian area, can only be compared with the thickly populated land between Osaka and Kobe in Japan.

According to my calculations, which are based on reliable statistics, there are nearly 4,500,000 surplus agricultural workers in Poland, but they are restricted to the former Austrian and Russian parts. Conditions in the former German areas are much better. Of course, Upper Silesia must be excepted, being mainly industrial.

The problem of this surplus population is one of the troubles with which the Warsaw government has to deal. As yet it has been unsolved. The attempts made to settle part of the surplus population in other parts, as in the new industrial area of Sandomierz, in the limits of the so-called Agrarian Reform, could hardly affect the question to any extent. Incidentally, the transferring of a part of the agrarian population to the towns helped to sharpen the Jewish question, for most of the trade is in the hands of the Jews, who are also well represented among craftsmen and even in the professions.

The types of farms and holdings vary with the density of the population. For example, while comparatively large farms are found in the more thinly populated districts, the areas with a surplus population contain mainly small holdings. These small holdings have been repeatedly divided and subdivided, until they have reached an almost incredible smallness. In some parts of Central Poland and Galicia, holdings under five acres make up 27% of the whole arable land. Again, conditions in this respect are much better in Posen and the Corridor. Not all the peasants in the former Russian and Austrian Poland are real farmers; many have adopted farming as an occupation, and are hardly able to maintain even the most humble existence. In West Poland, farmers enjoy a much better position. But something like 540,000 acres of agricultural property have already been broken up into small holdings in the more prosperous provinces. This measure was carried out as Agrarian Reform, but was really a question of the official minority policy, directed against the German-speaking population, who own much of the arable land there.

Modern agricultural methods are noticeable mainly in the former German provinces, while more primitive means are employed in the South and East, especially the latter. The purchasers of agricultural machinery and apparatus are mainly in the German parts of the country, so far as such equipment is imported at all. According to the intensifying of cultivation the price of agricultural products also varies. Better prices are paid in the West of Poland for vegetables, flax and fat products, partly on account of their better quality, and partly because traffic conditions are better, and sales more readily effected. But the low prices in East Poland have had a certain effect on those in the West, competitive rates being essential. The small holders in Galicia place their products on the market at a price which hardly enables them to purchase the necessities of life.

There is little industry in East Poland, with the exception of certain local undertakings and, perhaps, wood-working. Most of the industry in Central Poland is concentrated in Warsaw, but the armaments industry is domiciled chiefly in the Radom-Lublin-Kielce area, and there is also the new industrial centre of Sandomierz, already mentioned.

The textile industry of Lodz was adapted to the Russian market before the War, and has passed through many difficult phases, now mainly supplying British overseas areas, and thus displacing workers in Lancashire. The same applies to Bialystok, the second most important textile centre. Galicia has mainly ceramic factories, while the petroleum industry is also big; but the petroleum reserves of Boryslav and Drohobycz have been reduced considerably during the last twenty years, and fears are entertained that the supply will soon come to an end. Most of the industry is in West Poland, however.

Big industry lies in Upper Silesia. The ores are imported, largely from Russia and Sweden, but some of the world's richest deposits of lead and zinc are found there, while East Upper Silesia has big reserves of excellent coal.

The Sandomierz industrial centre would appear to have been established partly because Poland's other industrial areas are close to the frontiers.

Most of Poland plays a very unimportant part as customer. The best market is in the West, in the former German provinces. This is easily proved by Polish statistics. The consumption of coal per head of the population drops tremendously as one advances Eastwards. There are small holders in the East and South who practically live on their own products, or on such as they can obtain from their neighbours, being hardly able to buy even petroleum for lighting purposes. In some cases salt is actually a luxury, since it cannot be produced at home, but has to be purchased in return for cash.

While Poland is large in area, and contains a population of over 34 millions, it is not a potential market in the proper sense of the word, for only the inhabitants of the West really buy such goods as other countries have to sell. It is not only that the small holders have a low purchasing power; factory workers, minor officials, clerks, and the like, are hardly in a better position. Warsaw, a city of 1,200,000 inhabitants, and Lodz, with just half that number, are consumers of foreign products, but with those exceptions the market is in the West.

Polish industry has a fairly big capacity, while the home purchasing power is small, so that exports have to be fostered by every possible means. This applies particularly to the heavy industry and to the manufacture of textiles. The big industrial areas handed over to Poland after the War are too big for the country; their natural customers are separated from them by artificial frontiers.

To balance this, the Poles control export with the help of Government edicts, preference duties, export premiums, railway tariffs, and the like. Goods are sold far below the costs of production in many cases. This, again, is balanced by raising the price of industrial products in the home market, which, of course, makes it still harder for the people to buy. During the time when the German-Polish Agreement was in force, however, trading on the barter system was done.

The railway system also consists of patchwork, which is not surprising when one remembers that it is made up of parts of three railway systems. These three networks were only linked up at certain main points. While there are over 10 miles of railway per 100 square miles in Posen, 11.4 in the Corridor, and 18.5 in Upper Silesia, the other parts are poorly served. For example, voivodship of Warsaw has 5.2, Bialystok 4.2, and some areas even less miles of railway per 100 square miles. The Poles have built some railways since their Republic was founded, but these are mainly in connection with their newly founded port of Gdynia, while others are purely strategic.

The roads show similar contrasts. Motorisation makes little progress. In the Western part there were in 1938 3.3 cars per 1,000 of the population, while in the Eastern provinces there were no more than 0.3 cars per 1,000. There are 34.5 miles of consolidated roadway per 100 square miles of land in the West, 21.1 in Galicia, 13.5 in the former Russian provinces, and 3.2 in the East. The condition of the roads in the East is by no means good, although there are slightly better roads in Galicia. A few main highways through Central Poland are well maintained, but apart from them it is only in West Poland that good roadways are met with.

It will thus be seen that no economic improvements of importance have been made in Poland in the last 20 years. A new port has been fostered, and a certain amount of building has been done, but on the whole Poland is a backward nation. Even the rivers are neglected, very little commercial use being made of the Vistula. Conditions have not bettered since the War in what is now Poland. Certain progress has naturally been made as technique has advanced, but it is relatively slight as compared with that in other European lands.

3

Composition of Population

The population of Poland is 34,900,000 (excluding foreign residents), but one must not assume that there are as many Poles in that country. The inhabitants are made up of 7 million Ukrainians, some 2 million White Russians, 3,200,000 Jews, 1,500,000 Germans, and 200,000 Lithuanians, leaving 21,000,000 Poles. The Poles dominate., however, so that it may safely be assumed that many non-Poles record their national group as Polish in order to avoid difficulties, and that there are really much bigger minorities. One might perhaps put the number of Poles at 20 million without any fear of underestimating. The Jews are a minority, according to Polish statistics. This must not be regarded as my invention. Warsaw quotes them in this category. There were originally altogether 3,200,000 Germans in the area now composing Poland, of whom 1,700,000 left after the plebiscite in Upper Silesia owing to the oppression under the Poles. I quote more precise details of this modern migration of so many people in a later chapter.

The Ukrainians, the biggest minority, are only a part of a great nation overlooked or forgotten at Versailles. They proclaimed their independence, but it was short-lived. Their representatives at Versailles attracted no attention. Most of the Ukrainians live in Russia, a few in Rumania, and the rest in Poland. They differ in race and language from the Poles, with whom, indeed, they have nothing in common. The

White Russians are also Slavs, but also of a different group, while the Germans belong to the Teutonic race, and speak an absolutely different language.

The 1,500,000 Germans do not, of course, include the 400,000 in Danzig. Danzig comes in a different category, being entirely German. In fact, it is as German as Liverpool is English, and has a somewhat lower percentage of non-Germans than some English cities have of non-English.

It must not be forgotten that the German minority in Poland is only one of several. It would be a mistake to regard the German problem as the only one to be settled. Poland has never been a national State. Even in 1815, when she was divided with the express approval of France and Britain, there were non-Polish citizens within the country's boundaries, and minority problems existed.

It may safely be asserted that the repeated and long-drawn-out struggles between the minorities on the one hand, and the Poles on the other, led to the threefold partition of the country, robbing the State of its powers of resistance until the other countries had an easy task. In fact, dissolution seemed almost natural in view of the internal dissension. In each case, Russia was the driving force, so that it was interesting to learn that she was to guarantee Poland in 1939.

The Poles are not appealing to the world for the first time in history. I have already mentioned one previous example. But they forgot the lessons of history when their present State was founded.

The first official step towards the re-establishment of a new Polish State was taken by Germany, a fact often forgotten. Germany proclaimed Polish independence in 1916, and Pilsudski made a pact with the Reich before the War came to an end.

But, of course, Berlin had not intended to add such areas as Upper Silesia and the Corridor to Poland, or to found a new minority State. The Jewish minority of 3,200,000 is confessional, there being another half-million Jews of Christian religion. They thus make up ten per cent. of the entire population. In regarding them as a national minority, the

Poles are not alone, for this is general in Eastern Europe, including Rumania.

The bare figure does not convey the full significance of this group, 70% of the Jews residing in the towns, particularly of Central, East and South Poland. In Warsaw, for example, there are 820,000 Christians and over 350,000 Jews, the baptised Jews being included among the Christians.

There are thus more Jews in Warsaw alone than in the whole of Palestine. Lodz is the next biggest city with 400,000 Christians and 202,000 Jews. There are actually areas with a clear Jewish majority. In the Lublin province 44% of the inhabitants are Jewish, in the Bialystok province 38%, and in the province of Polesian, 49% are recorded as of the Hebrew faith. It is only in the towns which formerly belonged to Germany that there is a big majority of Christians.

The general standard of Jewish life is not upheld by the Jews of Poland. The Jews who left Germany and Austria were rich in comparison. Dirt and misery are the accompaniments. There are 250,000 Jewish craftsmen and 90,000 clerks, while the rest are either in business or act as agents, touts, and the like. Hundreds of thousands have no fixed occupation, but try to live on their wits. Many of them fail, presumably because the competition is too great. When a small number of citizens exercise their wits, they may be able to live comfortably, but when one-quarter of the population of a town attempts to make an existence in this manner, especially in a country where the general purchasing power is low, there is apt to be little opportunity for the individual.

The Jewish workers have a lower standard of living than their Polish colleagues, while the Jewish traders are, taken *en masse,* not to be compared with ordinary tradesmen elsewhere. They come into the same financial category as our street traders, and, as every police officer knows, most of these only carry a tray of wares to hide the fact that they are begging.

The streets of the Polish towns and villages are full of people with no visible means of support. Most of the Jews in this class collect rags, offer their services in an advisory capacity to any foreigners visible, carry a few pairs of bootlaces in their hands, or walk about with a little garlic which they hope to sell. In between they just hang about.

Many of the Jews go about dressed in a caftan and black cap of peculiar type. These usually live in ghettos which are of their own making, and they are the least disliked. Some are Zionists, while a fair percentage try to hide their Jewish characteristics and to pass as Poles. There are three unemployed Poles for each four at work, but statistics show that there are eight Jewish unemployed for each four with work.

The Jews welcomed the Polish State when it was founded. Pilsudski was not an anti-Semite. Some of the leading generals in the army are of Jewish origin, while not a few high officials have Jewish wives. Anti-Semites have only attained official importance since Pilsudski's death. The Poles have of late attacked the Jews wherever they could, but the Jews have parried most of the blows.

The White Russians are generally poorer than the Poles. They are Russian, but not Bolsheviks, and, although they are not satisfied with their situation in Poland, they do not desire to join Russia; that is, they are Russian in their feelings, but they do not wish to come under Soviet rule. They are mainly Greek Catholics, while the Poles are Roman Catholics. Their complaint is that they have not full facilities for teaching their children their own language. The Poles, who try to minimise the patchwork character of the country, do their best to assimilate this big minority, but they have not met with much success.

The Ukrainians make up the main minority. They are subjected to considerable difficulties and refuse to be assimilated. The Poles seldom give them passports if they can avoid it. Even when a Polish Ukrainian was appointed by his firm to act as representative in a big Continental capital recently, he was only given a passport valid for that one country. I examined this document myself.

The Ukrainians are the biggest nation without a country in the whole of Europe, but strangely enough their existence was unknown in Western Europe until the last half of the 19th century. Interest in them did not become general until after the Great War. An important feature of the Ukrainians is that they are settled in a compact area, largely in Russia; but the Galician districts of Stanislawow and Tarnopol are also almost entirely Ukrainian. They claim over 80,000 square miles in Poland, and in a part of this area, at least, they have resided since the fifth century. The Mongols massacred the Ukrainian inhabitants of the Eastern part of their realm, and burnt their capital, Kiev, in 1240. The Poles gained control of a part of the Ukrainian land in 1569, beginning a long series of brutal and oppressive acts. The Ukrainians were forbidden to talk of the former greatness of their people, or tell of their traditions. Many gave up their religion and nationality to avoid ruin. There were repeated revolts against the Poles, while the Tartars raided the Ukrainian areas periodically in search of booty and slaves. But the Ukrainians survived in some mysterious manner, making bows and arrows to defend themselves, and fighting with great tenacity. Autonomy and oppression alternated. What is regarded as luck for most peoples has proved a source of distress for the Ukrainians - their territory is rich, and other nations covet it, and have taken it. The Ukrainians now live in a state of subjugation in Poland, but they have their own organisation, and, seeing that they have withstood centuries of persecution, are not likely to abandon their hopes.

The German minority is equally subjected to oppressive methods, but its position is rather different. Whereas the Ukrainian and White Russian minorities lived in comparatively poor circumstances before the War, under the Czar, the Germans were prosperous. They were still the richest citizens when present Poland was founded.

There are German enclaves sprinkled all over Poland, but the main areas where they live are in the West, adjoining the Reich frontier, and in the Corridor. Their purchasing power is still relatively high, but they have been robbed of much of their land, and the process is still going on. They inhabit the richest areas which were handed to post-War Poland. Expropriation of the land is carried on with the ostensible object of assuring the landless of homes, and of adding to the extremely small holdings. In reality, however, little Polish and much German land is taken from big farmers. In Posen and the Corridor, for example, the Polish big-scale landed property has been reduced by 19% for the benefit of Polish settlers, while the German property was robbed of 63% of its area. Practically none but Poles are settled on the expropriated land. One reason for this measure is to obtain more Polish votes, and to reduce the percentage of Germans, in these areas. Despite all these measures, Posen and the Corridor are still predominantly German. In the Western provinces, some 50% of the children of Germans have no instruction in their own language, while in the Olsa district this figure is actually 88%. One school after the other has been closed by the authorities, in the hope that the coming generation will be compelled to speak only Polish, and thus be assimilated.

A fight is also waged against the Protestant Church, to which most of the Germans in Poland belong. Nearly all the Poles are Roman Catholics, but there are a few Protestants, and they have seized control of many of the German Protestant churches under various pretexts.

The Germans in the Corridor - and we must not forget that they make up the vast majority of the people there - are between two German provinces. On either side they see Germans who belong to the Reich, but they themselves are treated as second-class citizens. It is clear that they are dissatisfied. Their children often have to attend Polish schools, where they learn how Poland stretches ethnographically to Berlin. They form a solid block of Germans wedged in between the two parts of Germany, with the Baltic on the North, and the Poles in the South. But the officials who exercise control are Poles.

4

The Constitution

The Polish Constitution guarantees all citizens liberty of conscience, freedom of speech and right of assembly. This is not really allowed, of course. Newspapers are seized and speakers arrested. But the Constitution would be excellent, if only it were carried out. The Ukrainians and Germans suffer particularly owing to this. There are two chambers, the Sejm, or Diet, and the Senate. The Sejm consists of 208 deputies chosen by secret vote. The members of the Sejm are elected for a period of five years. Every citizen over the age of 21 has a vote. Taxes are fixed by the Sejm, which also legislates in general and performs the usual work of a Lower Chamber.

The Senate has 96 members, of whom 32 are nominated by the President himself; the remaining 64 are elected. The whole nation does not participate in this election. Only a select few may vote members to Senate. These include persons holding college diplomas, local government posts, and particularly privileged positions. Any person can be given the right to vote for the Senate if he is considered to be deserving. This means that the authorities exercise considerable power, even against the will of the people. No person under the age of 30 may have a Senate vote, while candidates for the Senate must be at least 40 years of age. It is hardly surprising under such circumstances that the minorities have not so much say in government affairs as they would have if both

Chambers were elected. This system is, no doubt, satisfactory to the Poles, but it reduces the rights of minorities still further.

The election of the President is not entirely democratic. The candidate is chosen by the assembly of electors. The Sejm selects fifty electors, and the Senate 25. The retiring President can, if he wishes, propose a further candidate. The new President is elected by a referendum. If, however, the retiring President does not make use of his privilege, the candidate proposed by the assembly of electors automatically takes office. The common people have thus only a very indirect say in the matter, for they have only participated in the election of the Sejm, which has only a share in the election of the President. It is clear that a mere 60% of the people would be unable to make their voices heard - if they were common people with no Senate vote. Small wonder that the minorities in Poland, which amount to "only" three-sevenths of the population, are seldom heard!

The President appoints the Premier, and also nominates the other members of the Cabinet, but this takes place on the recommendation of the Premier. The President has full powers to declare war without any reference whatever to the people, the Sejm, the Senate, the Premier or the other members of the Cabinet. As an individual, he may declare war in Poland's name whenever he pleases. Such is the clause in the Polish Constitution. He is furthermore head of all the armed forces of the State, and has power to ratify and to conclude treaties with other States. He can, of course, consult the members of the Cabinet on such matters, and generally does. But he is under no definite obligation to do so. He is thus a Dictator, and if he does not always make full use of his powers, it is merely because he prefers not to.

The Constitution is not the original one of post-War days, but dates back only to April 23rd, 1935. That is to say, the system of government was revised as from that date. The present government methods are partly based on those of Poland of several centuries ago, but with the addition of the vote for the Sejm for all persons over the age of 21, and with certain other modernisations.

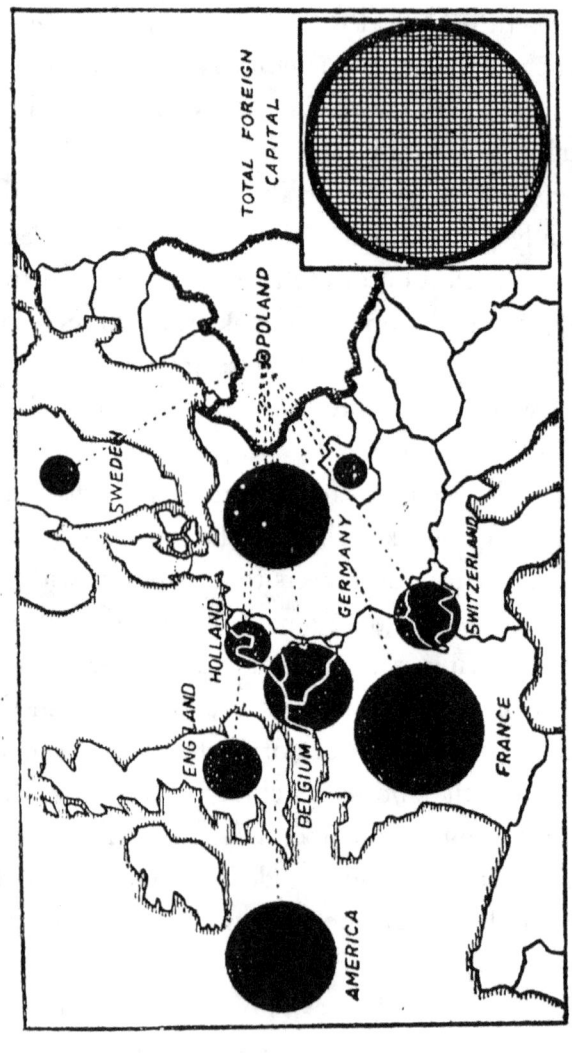

Foreign capital invested in Polish limited liability companies. The foreign capital invested in limited companies in Poland totals 1,446 million zloty, the participation of the different countries being as follows (in million zloty):

France   391   Germany   251   Switzerland 104   Holland 50   Bohemia-Moravia 23
America   277   Belgium   181   England   79   Sweden 39   Other lands   51

5

The problem of Danzig

It is impossible to deal with Poland without touching on Danzig, for this city has a customs union with Poland. Its citizens also have to permit their business abroad to be watched over by the Polish consulates, although, as Danzigers have repeatedly assured me, they prefer to send their passports to Danzig, for extensions or the like, by registered post rather than visit Polish consulates. This is not surprising.

As British subjects require a visa for Poland, I had to visit a consulate and, being in Berlin on my way to Warsaw, set out for the consulate there. I was unable to enter, for a big group of people were standing outside waiting. It seemed that the consulate was only open for two hours, which was not sufficient time for the work on hand, so many had to be turned away, but they remained in the road, hoping they might be let in later. Some were Poles, desiring endorsements of some kind, others persons seeking a visa, or making some enquiries. I only succeeded in entering because I went to the Embassy and asked for advice there. An official then immediately gave me a special endorsement on my form of application, which enabled me to obtain a Press visa, and on showing this document, I was admitted to the consulate. But if I were a Danziger, I should prefer to send my passport, since in any case the Embassy would not render me any assistance.

One of the claims of the Poles is that Danzig should not become part of Germany again on account of the Vistula. As has already been remarked on several occasions, a claim to the mouth of a river flowing through another country would mean that the Germans would have cause to quarrel with the Dutch about the Rhine. Strangely enough, the Germans never worry about the mouth of the Rhine being in Holland.

But the Vistula is not essential to Polish commerce. On the contrary, very little use is made of the river at all. Before the Great War, it was more utilised, although it was then divided between Germany and Russia, and the Russians did not foster commerce along it. In 1912, 610,286 tons of goods passed along the Vistula in either direction, as the lock figures show. That was not an exceptional year. On the contrary, in 1913 the figure was still higher, the total being 623,450 tons. But 20 years of progress in New Poland produced an astonishing result - in 1937 only 330,398 tons of merchandise passed along the Vistula. This is only a little over half the pre-War figure, so that any Polish claim to have made extensive use of the Vistula is obviously incorrect. The Poles say that the Vistula is necessary for their import and export business. Excluding transit trade, Poland had a turnover of 14,694,898 tons of merchandise which left or entered her frontiers by way of the Baltic in 1938. Of this total, only 453,851 tons passed along the Vistula!

The Poles claim that the Vistula is their main waterway, but only 453,851 tons of goods were carried along the river, or well under 10,000 tons per week, while more than 14 million tons arrived or left by way of the sea, but without touching the Vistula. No clearer proof could be wished for. The Vistula was of no great importance whatever in Poland's trade balance. In 1937 a mere total of 182,726 tons of goods were exported via the Vistula.

Of these only 30,163 tons, or 16.5 per cent. were from the interior of Poland, and not a single ton came from any place on the other side of Warsaw. Some of the goods came from East Prussia, incidentally. The Vistula has thus lost its importance as a connecting waterway between distant parts, although goods were transported along this river from much more distant areas before the War.

It was during the War that the Poles spread a statement to the effect that Danzig had a Polish majority. And the Poles made gallant attempts to realise this dream by fostering schools and associations. They established no less than 19 Polish kindergarten centres, while attempts were always made to persuade German parents to send their boys and girls there. The Association of Poles in Danzig has a membership of only 11,499, of whom no more than 7,561 are Danzig citizens, while the population of the Free City totals 407,517.

Danzig does not, of course, feel itself threatened by this small group. But, as a Free State, it is threatened by something very different. The Poles have done all in their power to foster Gdynia, and Danzig suffers accordingly. As preparations were completed in Gdynia, Danzig's trade dwindled. In 1926, 179 tons of goods were imported via Gdynia, and 640,696 tons by way of Danzig, the corresponding export figures being 413,826 and 5,659,604 tons. The total goods passing through Gdynia in 1926 were thus 414,005 tons, as compared with Danzig's 6,300,299 tons. By 1933 Gdynia's total had increased enormously to 6,105,866 tons, while Danzig's total fell to 5,152,975 tons. In 1929, to quote in percentages, 75.2% of the goods exported by way of the sea passed through Danzig and 24.8% through Gdynia; in 1933 Danzig's participation had fallen to 45.8%, and Gdynia's had risen to 54.2%.

Danzig thus sees its future threatened. Gdynia is to become, as Danzigers told me, Poland's future port, and Danzig is to have nothing. This, at least, is what the people think, and figures undoubtedly show that this is the tendency. For only less valuable goods are transported via Danzig. According to value, Danzig participated in 1938 to the tune of 7.5% of all Poland's imports, while Gdynia's share totalled 53.7%. Ores and gravel passed through Danzig.

The claim made by Marshal Rydz in a speech at Cracow on August 6th, 1939, was that Danzig was "Poland's lungs, as in one organism." This view is, however, difficult to uphold when the figures I have quoted are studied. Or, one might say, the speech should have been made before 1924, and is somewhat out of date - for the building of Gdynia made

Danzig a back-number. In reality, of course, Danzig never really earned this designation, but since 1924 it is an obvious misnomer.

There can be no doubt regarding the German character of Danzig. The earliest human settlement on the site of the present Free City dates back tens of centuries, but it is doubtful as to who actually founded it. The Romans, at the height of their success, referred to it as a trading centre. Certainly, there is no reason to believe that the founders were Polish. They may have been Slavonic, but it is equally likely that they were Germanic. The earliest settlement of which we have ethnographical records was Germanic, but a Slavonic tribe later settled there. Those Slavs were the Pomeranes, who were not Polish. Their present descendants are the Cashubes, a West Slav people. The city of Danzig was founded by Germans in or about 1224. Danzig flourished under the Teutonic Order. At the end of the 13th century Danzig belonged to the Hanseatic League. In 1454 the city passed from the Teutonic Order to the protection of the King of Poland, but remained a free Hanse City with a German administration. Neither Poles nor Jews might become Danzig citizens in those days. The city had its own economy, and even dabbled in foreign politics independently of Poland. Under Napoleon the French occupied the city, throttling its trade. This was part of the Little Corporal's scheme to blockade England, some assert, for, having failed to sweep the seas, Napoleon set about capturing the ports of Europe to prevent supplies reaching our shores.

Danzig was for long years part of Germany until the Great War. Following Versailles, the city was forcibly separated from the Reich, and the Poles laid claim to it. Their claim was based upon alleged historical rights, and upon the assertion that they need the whole course of the Vistula. After the War, one claim was that they needed the port, but since they have built Gdynia, no more has been heard of this. The Polish "minority" in Danzig may be compared with the negro "minority" in Cardiff - one does see some Poles in the former, just as one encounters representatives of the Dark Continent in the latter.

The claims of the Poles have increased of recent date, and they have recently been asserting that considerable areas in Germany, with a population between 95% and 100% Germans, should be handed over to them. Here and there, this view has been supported in the world Press, although it would be difficult to justify it.

But in the French Chamber, to quote one example, a very different view has often enough been taken. The session of the Paris Chamber on September 4th, 1919, is of considerable interest in this connection. The subject under discussion was the Peace Treaty and the terms implied. A report made by the Deputy, M. Charles Benoist, was being considered. Deputy Marcel Sembat made the following statement:

> "It must be openly admitted, as M. Charles Benoist has established, that Danzig is a German town. In order that there may be no doubt on the question, I shall read the text of his report on page 107:
>
>> "'Poland wanted to have Danzig. Nevertheless, from the simple point of view of the population, there is no doubt but that Danzig is an undisputedly German town. It is not a German enclave in Polish territory. One goes along the coast from Danzig through purely German land to East Prussia.'
>
> "Those are the words of the report. I do not hesitate to draw your attention clearly to the fact that there is a definite contradiction between the form in which we treat Danzig and the principles I have just mentioned. It is a question of a German town; we take it away from Germany. I know what you want to say to me, and I am of your opinion in advance. Poland must have access to the sea. I agree, and add that Danzig formed this access, offered to Poland by necessity."

That sums up the position. Danzig was admittedly German, but as there was no other port available for Poland, she was to have it - in some shape or form. The Poles, as I have already mentioned, have since proved that Danzig is not vital to them, for they now do most of their foreign trade by way of Gdynia. But there was no great port of Gdynia in those days. The Poles have developed it since, to cut out Danzig, thus showing that the reason given by M. Marcel Sembat was invalid. Or, at least, that it is no longer valid.

The *Daily Telegraph and Morning Post* published on July 3rd, 1939, an article by their former chief correspondent in Berlin, Mr. Hugh Carleton Greene. This article was headed: "Why a Free Danzig is Essential to Polish Independence." Mr. Greene sought to prove that Danzig should remain separated from the Reich, but he made considerable admissions - perhaps involuntarily.

He himself quotes a statement which he regards as inconvenient for German propagandists. Remarkably enough, his words support the view that Danzig is German. His exact words are as follows:

> "Danzig remained under the rule of the Knights until 1454 and was resettled by Germans. Since 1308 there has been no doubt about its 'German character.'
>
> "By 1454, when a union was concluded between Danzig and the Kingdom of Poland, the city was among the most prosperous ports of Northern Europe. This union lasted until the second partition of Poland in 1793 - an inconvenient fact which German propagandists are unable to explain away, although they insist, quite rightly, on Danzig's semi-independent position and control over her own affairs. Except for a short period as a Free State between 1807 and 1814, Danzig was from 1793 part of Prussia until the ratification of the Treaty of Versailles in January, 1920."

Mr. Greene's statements are correct, although he omits to mention that at the beginning of the 18th century Danzig was occupied by the French in an endeavour to throttle our trade. The main points he admits are that Danzig was German in character, and that it was "among the most prosperous ports of Northern Europe" at the time of the union with Poland in 1454. The Knights he refers to were the Teutonic Knights, and it is clear that under their control Danzig reached the prosperity Mr. Greene quotes. He does well not to mention the state of Danzig when the union with Poland came to an end, for the city was then anything but prosperous. Why German propagandists should try to explain away this union with Poland is not at all clear to me. But I agree that the union existed, but, as Mr. Greene also says, Danzig was semi-independent.

Mr. Greene also remarks in the course of his article that the solution was "not ideal" as was "shown by the conflicts between Poland and Danzig during the post-war years." This proves that the conflicts have nothing to do with the National Socialists, for there was no single Nazi in Danzig in those days. In claiming that Danzig should remain separated from the Reich, Mr. Greene still calls them "Danzig Germans."

The article in the *Daily Telegraph* sought to prove that Danzig is essential to Poland, and tried to stress the Polish origin of the city. It failed completely because if Mr. Greene quoted the actual facts, he drew the wrong conclusions from them. It is also mentioned that Danzig was inhabited by Slavs long centuries ago - but Mr. Greene wisely avoids the word "Poles." Slavs did live on the site of present Danzig - but they were not Poles.

To quote the 10th century to prove that Slavs lived in Danzig is, however, dangerous. Even assuming that they had been Poles (which they were not), the argument would not be nearly so good as that in favour of handing the United States of America back to the Red Indians now living in the Reserves, for they owned the country at a comparatively recent date, and there is no doubt whatever that they are the descendants of the former lords of the prairie.

The Slav claim to Danzig, even if founded (which is doubtful), dates back much further, though there is absolutely no proof (quite the contrary) that the Poles are the descendants of those Slavs.

If, however, a personal union with Poland long years ago entitles the Poles to claim Danzig, then I see no reason why we should not lay claim to Hanover - the whole province, not merely the town. Hanover and England were in a personal union from 1660 until 1837 - nearly two centuries. But I fear this proposal might work both ways. It was, after all, a Hanoverian (i.e. a German) prince, Georg-Ludwig by name, who assumed the title of George I of England, and came to London to rule over us as well as the Hanoverians. In other words, we were under German rule for well nigh two centuries. If a personal union enables the Poles to claim Danzig, the Germans might equally well claim England, Scotland and Ireland. The absurdity of such an argument must be obvious to anyone.

No such arguments as a personal union or the importance of the Vistula are valid. On the contrary, there is no reason whatever for regarding the Polish claim to Danzig as in any way tenable. Danzig can be the only judge as to whether it is German or not. The recent elections have clearly proved that the city is German in feeling, as it is in other respects.

It is true that the economic position of the Danzigers has not been bad of recent years, but this was due to the German-Polish Agreement, which assured the Free City a little business. Even so, the Poles avoided the real issue by more or less distributing the tonnage between Danzig and Gdynia, but arranging it so that the value of the goods going and coming via Gdynia should be greater, as figures already quoted prove.

Danzig has long since had a purely National Socialist Government, while the Danzig Radio Station is usually linked up with the Reich network. The Free State is too small to be able to arrange its own broadcast programmes on a big scale. To join the system with that of Poland would no doubt be welcomed in Warsaw, but it would have the drawback that none of the Danzigers would understand what was being said. There is no parallel with other small States. The only other State of small size with its own radio is Luxembourg, whose programme is intended mainly for British consumption, rather than for the local inhabitants.

The inhabitants of Danzig walk about with passports in their pockets. Indeed, they cannot go far without reaching a frontier. It is possible to go for a long walk in places, of course, but those who own cars must either travel abroad or drive in circles. Furthermore, such a small State is never independent in an economic sense, and foreign business is essential. Danzig business men have to go abroad to attend almost any conference - unless the other parties travel to Danzig, of course.

I was sharing a railway compartment in one of the Balkan countries with a Danziger not long ago, and we discussed the formalities necessary.

He told me that such formalities were quite impossible in Danzig, for if such forms had to be filled and so many questions were to be answered, a train would have crossed the second frontier before the formalities at the first had been settled.

As a Free State, Danzig is an artificial creation, which has no connection with earlier semi-independent or independent Free States. In earlier centuries small principalities and minute dukedoms were dotted all over Europe. Travelling was done by stage coach and it seemed to be quite a long way from one frontier to the other in any case. There were very different conditions to be dealt with. But to-day, such a small State is a nuisance to itself and others. It cannot be diplomatically represented, its currency is complicated, and the modern transport needs cannot be met. Danzig was a problem created in order to separate another group of Germans from the Reich. There was only one thing that was forgotten at Versailles - the Danzigers themselves should, in accordance with the much-vaunted principle of self-determination, have been asked to decide for themselves.

In order to show that these conclusions are not without the general support of well-informed persons and journals, I may quote the *Economist* of July 8th, 1939. An article endeavours to prove that the Poles are largely in the right, but the admissions made really prove the contrary. For example:

"But it would be wrong to think that the continued complaints from Danzig of Polish commercial policy and the serious effects of Gdynian competition are entirely unfounded. The structure of trade differs widely between the two ports; the predominant part played in Danzig by bulk goods of great weight but relatively small value makes total figures deceptive. Thus in 1937 Danzig exports, other than coal, which amounted to no less than 3.6 millions against 2.38 millions in 1936, decreased by nearly 200,000 tons...."

"In 1937, when the Free City was badly hit by Polish export restrictions on rye, barley and fodder, following the worst harvest in many years, it was hardly conducive to good feeling to find grain appearing in Gdynia, however modestly, as an export commodity...."

Another interesting quotation from the *Economist* of the same date runs:

"Danzig's losses are thus beyond dispute. The table printed below shows how strikingly the values of Poland's imports and exports through the two ports have changed." *[Scriptorium notes: see Appendix.]*

Professor Charles Sarolea has also written in support of Danzig. The Professor is known as a friend of Poland. He predicted the resurrection of that country in an article in *Everyman* as far back as 1912. In 1921 he wrote a book "for the special purpose of defending Poland against the systematic and unjust attacks of the British Press," to quote his own words. Three Polish translations were published, one by the Polish Foreign Office, which, incidentally, also published a Polish rendering of the Professor's "Impressions in Soviet Russia." Professor Sarolea prefaces his article, which appeared in the *Anglo-German Review* for July, 1939, with the words: "I am entitled to claim that I have always been a friend of Poland." He remarks that:

> "Our policy is indeed a paradoxical one. In order to punish Germany for her dismembership of Poland and Lithuania, we have made a military pact with Poland, that is to say, with the very government which, in 1920, initiated the dismemberment of Lithuania and the annexation of Wilno (Vilna), and which, in 1938, consummated the dismemberment of Czechoslovakia."

A further interesting quotation throws a new light on the whole situation:

> "Since the Polish State regained its independence, on at least five occasions it demonstrated its belief in the legitimacy of - and its allegiance to - power politics."

Examples follow, but they are similar to those I have already quoted. The Professor goes on to say that the minorities entrusted to Poland "transformed her from a homogeneous national state into a heterogeneous conglomerate of nationalities...."

Regarding Danzig, the same writer states:

> "Danzig is a purely German town. Ninety-five per cent of the population are Germans. So homogeneous a population is, in itself, sufficient to prove that Danzig always was a purely German town.... Nor, strangely enough, did the Polish people themselves ever try to settle in any large numbers in Danzig territory, so that a Polish minority problem never had any occasion to arise. It is, indeed, a curious anomaly, as was set out by the Editor of this Review in a recent article, that after 300 years of personal union

under the Polish kings and of close commercial intercourse, a much larger proportion of the Danzig population should have been of Scottish origin than of Polish origin."

This is explained by the fact, already quoted by myself, that the Poles were not allowed to become Danzig citizens during the personal union. But Professor Sarolea is unquestionably right - it is remarkable that there were more Scots than Poles in Danzig.

The Professor also deals with the question of access to the sea, and dismisses Poland's claims under this heading:

"As for the argument that Poland needs an outlet to the sea, in accordance with one of the fourteen principles of President Wilson, such an argument, which might have applied in 1918, no longer applies to-day, because the deliberate policy of the Polish Government has destroyed its validity...."

Lord Elton, speaking in the House of Lords in June, 1939, also raised doubts as to the justice of Danzig's position. His precise words were as follows:

"All I should like to ask is: Have His Majesty's Government any sort of contact with the German Government on the question of Danzig, or has that question been relegated for the moment owing to its inflammatory character, or for other reasons, to the category of the untouchable?"

This was much to the point, for the very mention of Danzig's German character has been all but ruled as out of order.

According to the *Gazetta del Popolo* of Turin (No. 160), "Hitler will come into possession of Danzig as surely as the sun will rise to-morrow morning." This journal was of the opinion that no Anglo-French veto would make any greater impression than in Autumn, 1938. Incidentally,

Mussolini warned the Poles to moderate their attitude long years before the Axis was thought of.

The Danzig problem was created at Versailles. Dean Inge went further than this in the *Church of England Newspaper* (July 7th, 1939, front page), when he remarked that "the things which we hate in Germany are largely the creation of the Allies, especially France, after the peace. If we had made things easier for the Weimar Republic there might have been no Nazism."

It would be fitting to revise these clauses which have never met with the approval of thinking Britons ever since the Treaty of Versailles has existed. But it would have been much better if we had revised this treaty, and met the just demands of the minorities, before Germany rearmed - in the days of the Weimar Republic.

The *London Evening Standard* (June 19th, 1939) published an article by George Malcolm Thomson, in which the terms of the Peace Treaty were sharply criticised. The heading ran: "Nobody wants to fight for Danzig." The article gives some interesting details, of which I quote a few extracts:

> "Certainly, it should not be hard to make a better settlement than the Peace Treaty imposed on Danzig. By the time the negotiations were over, Danzig found itself with four separate constitutions, and five or six different ruling authorities. It became a Free City under the League. Its domestic affairs were controlled by the Danzig Senate, its foreign relations by the Polish Government. But there were complications.
>
> "If you boarded a train in Danzig, you came under the jurisdiction of the Poles. For the railways were Polish. If you got on a tramcar, on the other hand, you were looked after by the Free City.... If you had business to do in Danzig harbour, you came under the Harbour Board. And that was a half-and-half body, partly Danzig, partly Polish, with a Swiss chairman.... When a Danzig citizen wanted a passport, he had to apply to Warsaw.

When the city proposed to raise a loan, again it had to apply for permission to Warsaw. The Poles generally gave the passport, but they did not always consent to the loan.

"At any rate, for a whole year they held up a loan for harbour improvements. And during that year, the Danzigers allege, the Poles pushed ahead with the construction of their new port of Gdynia, on the Baltic....

"...to make the financial tangle worse, the Free City was cursed with two currencies. The Danzig gulden and the Polish zloty. Both were legal tender. You could use either... on the tram. But when you took the train you had to pay for your ticket in Polish currency."

In the same article, Poland is warned not to regard Danzig as "a flag which, if hauled down, would damage Poland's prestige and inflict injury on the nations acting in support of Poland."

The description of the complications may serve to explain why Danzigers were against having a "Free City" from the start. Other States have one central government, but the "Free" part of Danzig consisted of having several authorities and other complications. Mr. Thomson's article also makes it clear that Danzig is not a military basis, as so many people wrongly believe. He writes, "...Danzig is not a military objective that wise generals would choose to fight for." He also says that "if the Poles, defying Hitler, marched into Danzig, they would pay dearly for their rashness."

As regards the High Commissioner, the same article remarks that he cost £44,000 per annum at first, but that he "does not appear often in the city" nowadays.

The concluding paragraph of this article also deserves quotation. It runs:

"But the sensible plan would be to recognise the national spirit of the German population and, on that basis, to make a new accommodation between Polish and German claims. The Poles have much less to fear from a Danzig where the citizens dwell in contentment than from a city whose people feel themselves deprived of a national right and subject to form of administration which they find irksome."

The statements regarding Danzig and Gdynia are proved by official Polish figures. Each year after 1924, the new port was extended or improved, and it is obvious that the right to refuse the Free City permission to raise a loan to improve the harbour was to the advantage of Gdynia. It is such matters that have made the Danzigers regard the Poles as their competitors, and not as their friends and helpers.

It has been authoritatively asserted in England that Danzig was not included in the Reich when the peace treaties were made because a foreign Power holding the delta of the Vistula could blockade Poland and economically strangle that country. Now if this is so, the argument I have already quoted regarding the Rhine might be pressed by Germany as meaning that the independence of the Reich was in danger because the mouth of the Rhine is in Holland. The Danube question might be similarly dealt with. The argument sounds outwardly feasible to those who have never left Britain's shores, and who only know their rivers as entirely British. But such blessings are enjoyed by few other lands. The Danube is shared by numerous countries, including Germany and Hungary, and its tributaries extend through wide tracks of S. E. Europe. But certain East Prussian villages were included in Polish territory, and not allowed to participate in a plebiscite, so as to make the Vistula all-Polish. This was probably the first time in Europe that villages were handed over to a foreign Power merely in order to keep the banks of a river in one State. It created a very dangerous precedent.

As at that time Germany's army was restricted to 100,000 men, and no heavy arms were permitted her, it is difficult to see how she could have blockaded Poland, especially since the warships to accomplish such a task had been sunk at Scapa Flow. But to-day Germany could blockade

Poland. The Polish coast is some 50 miles in length, and a small part of the German navy could accomplish this task with ease, as every strategist will admit. We thus see that the possession of Danzig is not necessary for a blockade.

I have quoted figures to show how the Poles have gradually withdrawn their trade from Danzig, and have shown that the value of the merchandise is sinking from year to year. [Scriptorium notes: see Appendix.] A further example may help to make the situation clearer. The value per ton of the goods passing through Danzig in 1938 was 62.8 zloty, that of goods entering or leaving Gdynia totalled 116.7 zloty per ton. It must also be remembered that Danzig depreciated its currency largely with the object of coming into line with the zloty (in 1935). But trade only enjoyed a brief benefit as a result. That Danzig retained a part of its export trade was mainly due to foreign firms, who preferred dealing with Danzigers. Communication was easier, for example. In fact, imports via Danzig actually increased between 1934 and 1938 to a much greater degree than those going through Gdynia. In the same period, exports through Gdynia grew tremendously, mainly because the Polish authorities, in granting licences, favoured the port they had built. Imports in 1934 via Danzig totalled 655,763 tons, via Gdynia, 991,544 tons; by 1938 Danzig was responsible for 1,547,866 tons, and Gdynia for 1,526,536 tons. And yet Danzig's total trade was only 7,131,752 tons, against Gdynia's 9,173,438 tons.

Those who allotted Danzig to Poland's customs union naturally believed that the Free City would remain Poland's sole port. Indeed, the Poles had claimed it because they needed a port. Wilson and Lloyd George would never have agreed to this if the Poles had announced their intention of building a rival port to undermine Danzig's trade. It is true that Warsaw accorded Danzig a comparatively recent agreement, assuring the Free City of a full share in trade. But there was no improvement in the situation - on the contrary, immediately afterwards Danzig's share in the trade fell again, this time from 26 to 24% (in 1937).

Danzig developed industries to balance the growing loss of trade, but Poland placed a high duty on machines and machine parts. This was a purely one-sided arrangement. There was a time when the number of unemployed in Danzig totalled 40,000, which is a figure corresponding to nearly four and a half million registered unemployed in Great Britain. Danzig cannot be said to be extremely prosperous to-day, but what the city has is due to orders from Germany. The shipyard, especially, is kept busy with German orders, while Zoppot and the spas live mainly on German visitors.

The Vistula is one of the five great streams of Europe, and might reasonably be expected to have proved the pride of Poland. But the river loses in importance from year to year.

All this, so long as it applies to the Vistula in Polish territory, is, of course, the business of the Poles alone. If they prefer to neglect their great river, it is not for us to complain. But it is unjust for German land to be included in Poland, and for Danzig to remain outside the Reich, in order to assure the Poles an all-Polish river which they themselves neglect, and which is not, as generally assumed, their main artery of commerce at all.

Danzig has its own Senate, a High Commissioner appointed by the League of Nations, and a Polish High Commissioner in residence. The members of the Senate are elected by the adult population of these 750 square miles of territory forming the Free City.

But the High Commissioner appointed by the League takes no active part nowadays, while, according to Mr. George Bilainkin, the author of "Poland's Destiny," "the resident Polish High Commissioner is also ignored." Bilainkin, in the *Sunday Press* (July 16th, 1939) wrote that "Danzig's German citizens - and they are admittedly in a vast majority - have every possible opportunity of exercising complete Germanism." Bilainkin also writes of Danzig that "already Nazi flags fly from all houses." And his article aims at proving that Danzig must remain outside the Reich. Yet he cannot avoid making these important admissions.

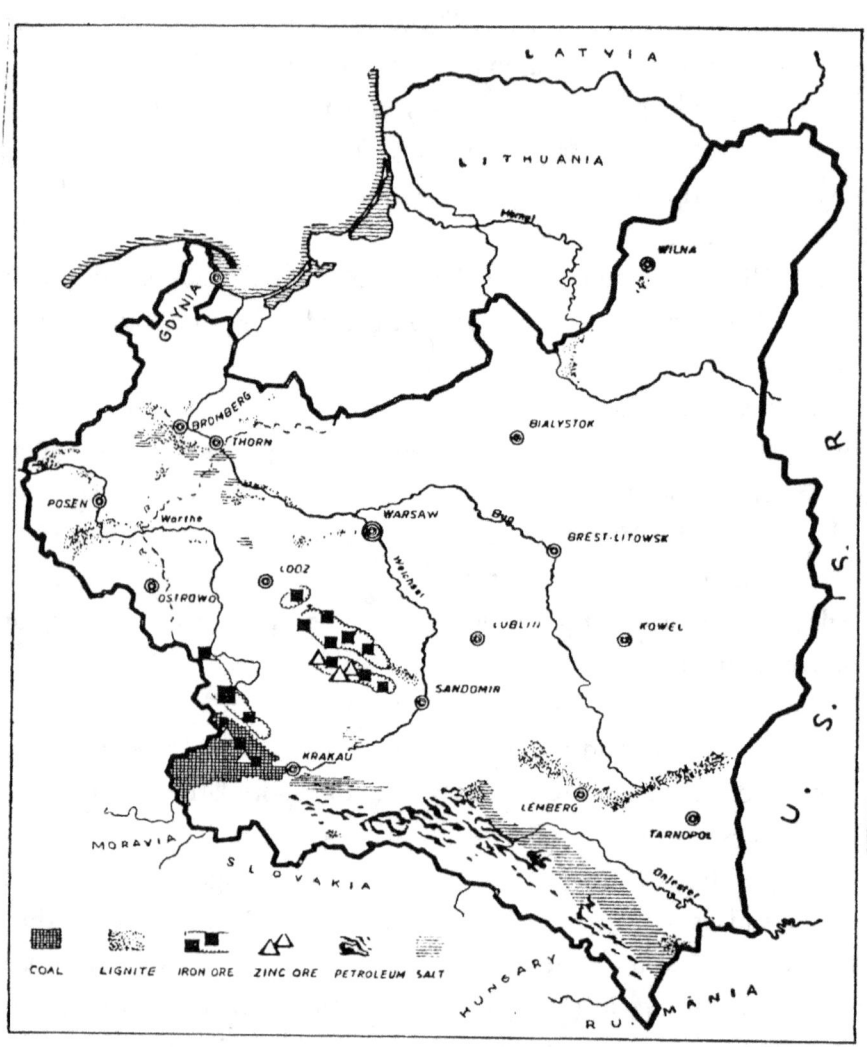

The distribution of mineral wealth in Poland.

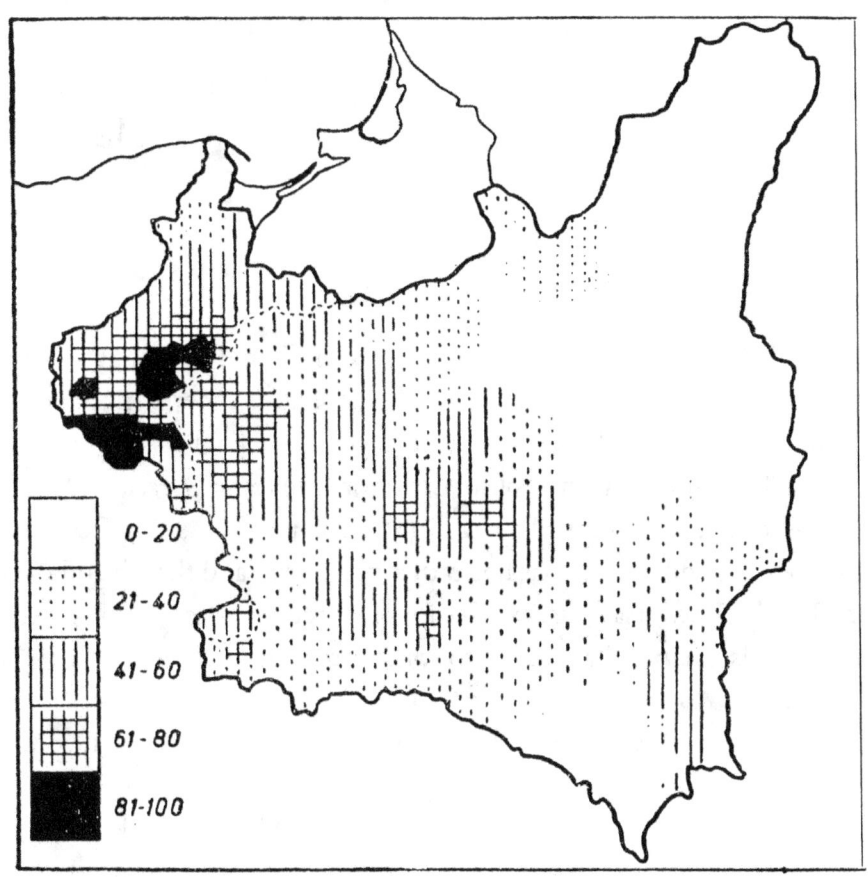

The agrarian productivity of Poland.

(Based on the harvests of the main agrarian products, according to Ornicki " Wladomosci geograficznych ").

6

On tour in Poland

Travelling in Poland is extremely interesting. But it is not like visiting one single country. The tourist who sees Poland is experiencing a tour through a number of lands, and this was what one Englishman I met in Gdynia liked most. In the Polish Corridor, in Upper Silesia, and, to a slightly lesser extent, in the Province of Posen, it is like visiting Germany - but with the difference that it is rather old-world, and that the officials are Polish. In Warsaw, as well as in the broad territory East of the capital, it is like pre-War Russia to some extent; in the South-West it is like pre-War Austria with some variations. There are also other different territories, but these are the three most notable. One could trace the former map of Europe by 'taste,' strange as that may seem. For example, we may take three cities - Posen, Warsaw and Cracow. In Posen, the food is much the same as in Berlin to this day. Even the vegetables are cooked with flour (a method I detest), just as in Prussia. This, of course, is a matter of taste - but the tastes of Posen and Berlin agree. Warsaw has very good cooking. One must go to a good restaurant, the smaller ones being none too clean. But the cuisine is good. There is the excellent cooking of Czarist Russia in the main. Cracow has good pastries, like Vienna, and the coffee is served with a big portion of whipped cream, as customary in Austria.

Of course, the cuisine is not conclusive. I merely mention it by the way. But the character of each part of Poland varies in the same manner.

To abide by these three cities as examples, Posen is clearly German by origin. The Exhibition Building of which the Poles are so proud was built by Germans - but the Poles told me that they had kept it in repair and added to it. They agreed that the main building was German, however. The main hospital is German - but they hastened to inform me that they had added a wing to it. The famous Poznan (Posen) Fair is held in a building mainly built by the Germans. In fact, a drive in a cab through the town of Posen will convince anyone who knows Germany that the architecture is the same. The flats are much the same as in towns of corresponding size in all parts of Germany. The people speak as much German as Polish. In fact, I failed to discover a single adult civilian who did not speak German, and I purposely addressed scores of people in the streets, asking the way or the time. Children, however, did not understand in many cases, and several officials were unable to grasp what I meant. One hears more Polish than German in the streets, but many of these people speak German when alone. I know this because, once they had chatted with me and seen my British passport, they told me openly that they found it better not to speak German in public in view of the trouble which might result. Most remarkable of all was a purely Polish cab-driver who told me with tears in his eyes of what the town was like before it became Polish. He spoke fairly good German, had enthusiastically greeted the establishment of modern Poland, but has been disappointed. "It is not as it was," he repeated again and again. The hotels were empty. I could choose rooms of any desired size and on any floor. These hotels were built when the city was German, and were to accommodate more guests than ever arrive nowadays, excluding the time of the Fair.

Warsaw has what I consider to be a real Polish atmosphere, but with a close resemblance to pre-War Russia as I remember it as a child, when my father once took me there. The streets are full of horse-drawn cabs. True, many taxis have also appeared, but they have less custom. In Warsaw there are also minorities, of course, but the Poles really predominate. It is mainly Russian-built, but the population is chiefly Polish.

The Jewish minority is large. The Jews do not, as a rule, mix much with the Poles (there are naturally numerous exceptions to this rule) but live in a ghetto. This ghetto must not be compared with Whitechapel, for the latter is modest in contrast. Warsaw's ghetto is a pre-War Russian ghetto in character. The men are to be seen with beards, the youths never appear to begin shaving at all, both wear long black coats (even in the hottest weather) and black skull-caps. They speak more Yiddish than Polish, and I discussed different topics with a group of them at one street-corner, using the best Yiddish at my command. I may remark that I understand this jargon well, but speak it haltingly. I cannot, however, read it when it is written by hand. It is read from right to left, and is inscribed in Hebrew characters. It contains very little Hebrew, beyond the religious expressions, contrary to popular belief.

Religious ceremonies are not only held in the many synagogues, but also in make-shift rooms, often in the basement, but with the windows open. From the narrow lanes one can often see the Oriental ceremonies. I watched two such ceremonies from outside the windows.

There are many splendid buildings dating back to the days of the old kings of Poland. In former days the Poles clearly erected excellent monuments to their age, but it is remarkable that little has been accomplished in this respect since new Poland has existed. The very presence of these old buildings lends Warsaw a real Polish atmosphere, which differs so much from the Corridor, Upper Silesia, Vilna, Posen, White Russia and Olsa. For the real Poland was of moderate size, while the present State is the fifth largest country in Europe.

Cracow was once the capital of Poland, and is the oldest and most beautiful city in the country. Most of the people know German, and there are several big minorities. One can accost any passer-by in German and the chances are ten to one that he answers in the same language. But when I went into the official Polish Tourist Bureau at Cracow, I found no one spoke a single word of English or German, and only one girl knew French. A guide speaking any one of these languages could not, I was told regretfully, be obtained, no matter how much I paid. Of course, I was informed, in another month, or a week later, something might be done, but not on that day. As there was no object in engaging a Polish-speaking guide (for if I had to use my bad Polish I could talk with the keepers and watchmen just as well), I made my tour alone. But it was strange in a town formerly part of Austria, and where thousands of unemployed are seen in the streets, that no one speaking any language but Polish could be found as a guide. I am unable to believe that this is really the case. My belief was later confirmed at Kattowitz, where I went into the Polish travel bureau, and no one was, even after I showed my passport, prepared to speak anything but Polish, while in the streets more people understand German than Polish. Indeed, the town is almost entirely German - but officially only Polish is understood.

Wieliczka is an especially good example. This is a small town about 10 miles from Cracow, and contains what are probably the largest salt mines in Europe. It is true that tradition says that the mines were started on the initiative of a Hungarian princess, but this town is now mainly Polish, and in no case Hungarian. The salt mine is much advertised. In any Polish travel bureau, whether in London, Paris or New York, one obtains booklets on it in English. But on arrival, one finds that not a single guide there will speak any language but Polish. I tried every guide present. Only Polish answers were given. In this respect Poland is unique. No other country in Europe advertises its sights in several languages but provides no interpreter-guides. Only a minority complex could lead to such a state of affairs. Incidentally, the mines contain vast halls with salt floors, walls and roofs, with carved salt figures, mainly of religious subjects. One chamber is over two centuries old, while another, named after the late Marshal Pilsudski, is nearly 450 feet below the earth.

Gdynia contains mainly Polish edifices. This was a small place in 1920, but the Poles have turned it into a port, apparently in order to prevent their trade from passing through Danzig. This is the one city of Polish and modern design. If the Poles intended to adhere to their customs union with Danzig, it was unnecessary to build this new port at all. Obviously they considered that this customs union would cease to exist sooner or later. It is interesting to note that this city was built by the Poles long before the National Socialists came to power in Germany, so that they obviously had nothing to do with it. Gdynia's population, according to "Poland," a booklet published in 1937 by the *Liga Popierania Turystyki* (League for Promotion of Tourism) at Warsaw, increased from 2,000 to 110,000 in the course of the ten years preceding the issue of this booklet. Most of the 108,000 new inhabitants are 100 per cent. Poles. Almost all the 2,000 were Germans. The building of a port here thus served a second purpose - it provided a majority of Poles in the town previously all German, and it increased the percentage of Poles in the Corridor artificially. To balance this, other building has been sadly neglected in Poland. The Corridor is still predominantly German, and even such big-scale attempts to settle Poles there have had little effect on the general position. But the experiment is interesting and enables Poland to point to one Polish-built town on the Baltic.

I saw little evidence of big shipping. Indeed, the Poles are not enthusiastic seamen, which one readily understands. They have always been an agricultural nation, all through history. They have some industries, mainly intended for supplying the home market or their immediate neighbours, but agriculture is their main stand-by. Unlike the British, Dutch, Germans and Spaniards, to mention but a few, they never participated in overseas trade. Who has not read in books - or learnt at school of the Spanish merchant ships or the Dutch fleet, or the vessels which set out from Hamburg and Bremen? Who has not also heard of French, Portuguese, Norwegian, and other ships in early days? But no one can find a single trace of any Polish seafaring activities. The reason is that there were none. Polish seafaring began after the Great War, and has developed very little since. The Polish navy is one of the smallest in Europe.

On paper, the Poles have everything. But I soon discovered that it was only on paper. For example, I was told I could conveniently fly from Warsaw to Gdynia in about 1¼ hours. One can, there is no doubt, when one has an aeroplane at one's disposal. But when I went to Cook's, they said I should have to wait till the next day. I could, however, fly the next morning. They noted my name, my hotel, worked the price out for me in English money, and I began to pay. The clerk then had an idea. He said he would just phone to make sure that accommodation was free. It was not. We changed the time. I was to fly on Sunday afternoon. After all details were arranged, he had another idea, and consulted the timetable, only to discover that there was no service on Sunday afternoons. We fixed Monday, but the seats proved to be sold out. I ultimately reached Gdynia, but it was only by good luck.

This is not an isolated example. I could quote dozens. There is the famous Torpedo, the railcar between Warsaw and Cracow, which travels 362 kilometres (some 225 miles) in four hours. It seats between 50 and 60 people, and has several stops on the way. I was told I should have to pay extra for a reserved seat. I did so, but when I got in I found there was no seat at all, reserved or otherwise. On the contrary, everyone had such a ticket, and dozens of people were standing, particularly ladies and older people. On another occasion I watched this train start. There was what might almost be described as a free fight to get in. Porters blocked one door putting the luggage in the small compartment in front, while men and women fought to get in first. The weaker had to step back and the stronger reserved seats for themselves.

The aeroplanes exist, so do the railcars, but it is the exception rather than the rule if one is able to make use of them.

The Warsaw authorities are trying to abolish the one really adequate and interesting means of locomotion in the city, the old-fashioned cab. The people oppose this strongly.

In summer, 1939, I found the Poles had very little change; this came to my notice on my first day in Warsaw, when 12 zloty were handed to me when I paid a bill for 8 zloty. I received 24 small coins. The Poles asserted that the Jewish minority had collected all the silver coins, especially the 5- and 10-zloty pieces, so that they had no coins except those of the lowest denomination. I was told that the best way to deal with this hoarding would be to withdraw all silver coins from circulation, and some said that this was already planned, and that 10-zloty notes were to be printed. Rumours of various kinds were rife, and there was talk in the middle of July of inflation.

While tourists are invited by prospectus to visit Poland, they are taxed when they arrive. A visa costs 25 zloty, and there is a daily tax. Motorists are taxed 1 zloty per day for the upkeep of the roads, although certain motoring associations have secured exceptions for their members. I met a Scotsman and his wife in Warsaw, and their car had suffered considerably, they told me, owing to the bad state of the roads. Between Gdynia and Warsaw, and around Plock, they assured me the roads were among the worst they had ever seen in their lives.

I saw no signs of any foreign tourists in any of the smaller towns, not even in Cracow, where the ancient buildings and city walls might be expected to attract visitors from all parts of the world.

7

A Nationality State

There is no doubt that Poland is a State of nationalities, as the Poles themselves readily admitted until this summer. This view is also expressed in the Polish publication *Poland Old and New* by Joseph Statkowski (Arct, Warsaw, 1938), intended for English consumption, and printed in English. On page 107 M. Statkowski says that the "largest national minorities in Poland are the Ukrainians," and he quotes some figures to show what a big percentage they form.

The writer admits that there are 70% Ukrainians in the voyvodship of Stanislawow, and the same number in that of Volhynia. Actually, the percentage is much higher; the object of *Poland Old and New* is to defend Greater Poland. The book is prefaced by a map showing the Slav tribes as formerly extending as far as the present Danish-German frontier. But the author also admits that the Ukrainians form a compact minority, for he remarks that "the majority of the Ukrainians inhabit the south-eastern provinces of Poland." Even in Tarnopol, he adds, 46% of the inhabitants are Ukrainian. He estimates the natural increase of the Jews in Poland at 50,000 a year, and admits that "the excess Jewish population is finding it gradually more and more difficult to get a livelihood," while the "economic problems of the peasants" and the "continued crisis in agriculture" have "brought the Jewish question in the villages into a greater prominence than ever."

In one week I saw five cases of Jews being arrested in Warsaw, and it must be remembered that most Jews live in their own districts, where I only spent a matter of some hours.

M. Statkowski agrees that there is a "White Ruthenian" national minority (referred to by me as White Russians, to prevent confusion with the Ukrainians, who are also called Ruthenians, but without the prefix "White"), but he estimates it as only 1,500,000, and adds that there are "less than 90,000 Lithuanians." It will thus be seen that even nationalist Polish writers (I have quoted a typical example) do not deny the existence of large minorities, although they do try to minimise their importance. The same writer says that most of the Germans "left Poland of their own free will when this country regained her independence," and that there are at present "about 200,000 Germans in Poznania (Posen)." This number is well underestimated, but the admission that most of the Germans left when the provinces fell under Polish rule is illuminating.

There were actually some 2,500,000 Germans in the former German provinces awarded to Poland, but a big percentage left. A few, no doubt, did so of their own free will, rather than become Polish citizens, but the majority left because they were subjected to petty annoyances, in some cases, and actual persecution, in others. Their land was taken in the manner already described, many of their schools were closed; their organisations were declared illegal, and they were debarred from working in many walks of life. Official positions were practically impossible to obtain. Often enough, it was considered an offence for Germans to chat in the streets in their own language.

I gave special attention to this point in Kattowitz, which is mainly German to this day. Walking quickly through the streets, I heard Polish being spoken here and there, but not a sound of German reached my ears. I then strolled slowly along, listening attentively, and I heard German being spoken in undertones. Whilst the Poles chatted loudly, the Germans spoke in undertones. I approached a group of four people talking German quietly and their conversation ceased. Again, on one of the squares, where there are many seats, I sat down, and the conversation ceased. One young couple exchanged a few words of - broken Polish. I turned to three young men on the other side of my seat and asked them in German the name of the square, adding that I was English. Smiles of relief were noticeable, nods exchanged, and low voices began talking German again. My new friends explained that talking German led to trouble; they would be asked questions, perhaps even arrested. One of them had a German novel - absolutely non-political - with him, but it was in a Polish paper cover, so that no one might notice he was reading German. In 1938 there were 107 German periodicals published in Poland, and the number is still round about a hundred, all of which sell reasonably well, but one seldom sees people reading them - unless it is in their own homes.

There were no less than 122 Ukrainian publications in Poland in the same year and the figure remains steady.

Poland Old and New is a semi-official Polish publication, and when even such a book had to admit that Poland is a "nationality State," it would be difficult for others to deny it.

Other German towns include Königshütte and Oderberg, while the Olsa area is Slovakian. This was, for some reason which I am unable to explain, awarded to the Poles, but was included in Czecho-Slovakia when the latter was founded after the War. The population is not Polish but Slovak. Possibly the mistake arose owing to the fact that the population is not Czech, so that it was supposed to be Polish. This, of course, affects only that part of Poland added to the realm in 1938.

A glance at the historical maps of almost any encyclopaedia shows that Poland had never had a coast-line. In the middle of the 14th century, for instance, Thorn was a northern frontier town of Poland, the Corridor belonging to the Teutonic Knights, who were, as the Poles themselves admit, German. Upper Silesia was even then German. Pomerania, however, was once under Polish sovereignty, but only for a brief period.

General statements about the Polish Corridor, and Danzig in particular, seem only to be made by those who have never been there. Those who have visited these areas speak very differently. Sir Arnold Wilson, M.P., in *The Times* of July 7th, 1939, referred to his tour of Danzig and the Sudetenland as follows:

> "Some of your readers may care to hear something of the impressions left on my mind by a recent visit to parts of the Sudeten district of Germany and (last Sunday) to Danzig; there is calm at the centre of the cyclone and after a day spent there in the company of well-informed foreign as well as German residents, I scarcely recognise the picture painted in certain London Sunday and other newspapers which any Berliner can buy and whose lurid contents sufficiently explain the widespread belief abroad that Londoners are a prey to vain fears spread by occult influences."

The *Daily Sketch* recently stated that "no credence can be attached" to the rumours regarding Germany and Danzig. Dean Inge has written some interesting facts in the *Church of England Newspaper,* one quotation being as follows:

> "Versailles had to be revised, with or without war. Hitler is trying to do it without war. He cannot be allowed to have everything his own way; but are we going to fight about Danzig, a thoroughly German town, which never ought to have been separated from the Reich?... Let us cease from the childish habit of personifying other nations as monsters."

According to *The Times* (July 12th, 1939), the *Deutsche diplomatisch-politische Korrespondenz,* official mouthpiece of the German Foreign Office, wrote that "The German solution to the Danzig question has always been regarded by the Reich as a peaceful solution in which the interests of the harbour as well as of its hinterland would be secured to mutual advantage. So far as a possible danger to the Polish access to the sea in case of conflict is concerned, nobody, and least of all in England - where claim is still made to some understanding about blockades - will seriously accept that with or without Danzig Germany would not then be in a position to shut Poland off hermetically from the sea. The settlement of the Danzig question, however, should, in the German view, have excluded such eventualities for ever."

In a leading article of the same date *The Times* clearly stated that "British interests are not the least involved in the local issue, and neither in Great Britain nor France could it possibly be a popular battle-cry to 'fight for Danzig.'"

Years ago British attacks on Polish chauvinism were the order of the day. H. G. Wells in *The Shape of Things to Come* wrote of the restoration of Poland, but regretted that "instead of a fine, spirited and generous people there appeared a narrowly patriotic government which presently developed into an aggressive, vindictive and pitiless dictatorship." These are hard words, but Mr. Wells went on to say that the "most disastrous of all the follies of Versailles was the creation of the Free City of Danzig and what was called the Polish Corridor."

Marshal Foch, too, interested himself in this problem, claiming that the "Corridor area will be the cause of the next war."

Sir Arnold Wilson has been in Danzig three times during the last four years. I have already quoted the opening of his letter to *The Times*. This letter contains some further passages worthy of attention. For example, writing of progress in Danzig, he says:

> "...I have watched the slow but natural process of 'reversion to type' which is now complete. It is once more what it was in 1919, a microcosm of that part of Prussia to which it belongs geographically and racially. The will to revert to Germany is, for whatever reason, as strong as it was in the Saarland before the plebiscite. Whatever the merits of the status quo of 1919, its

moral basis has disappeared. The principle employment is not transit trade but shipbuilding, which is very active. Some yards are working three shifts; all slips are full. All orders come from or through Germany. But the importance of Danzig to Poland remains; Danzig can be blown to pieces from Gdynia, and vice versa. The treatymakers of Versailles intended that Danzig should be Poland's only outlet to the Baltic; Gdynia was made only because Danzigers in 1922, actively encouraged in every possible way by the British Labour Party, prevented the transit of arms needed by Poland to resist Russian aggression which they not merely condoned but applauded.

"Herr Hitler stated on April 18 that he had proposed to Poland that Danzig should be incorporated within the Reich as a Free State (Staat). The phrase implies the continued existence of the Free Port in Danzig harbour (such as exists in Hamburg and Trieste); it also implies the absence of guns and fortifications on this sector of the Polish frontier.

"Here is the basis of a settlement, if Germany could satisfy Poland that the natural desire for a corridor across Pomorze is not the precursor of a demand for Pomorze and Posen.... In Danzig at the moment there is more fear of a Polish than of a German coup. Memories of the very recent Polish descent on Teschen and Oderberg, of the Vilna coup, and of the exploits of Korfanty are as vivid as Tannenberg...."

On April 2nd, 1917, the late President Wilson made his celebrated speech before Congress. Almost everything he said is a complete refutation of the idea of including German areas in a non-German country. For example, towards the end of his speech, he solemnly stated:

"We are glad, now that we see the facts with no veil of false pretence about them, to fight thus for the ultimate peace of the world and for the liberation of its peoples, the German peoples included: for the rights of nations great and small and the privilege of men everywhere to choose their way of life and of obedience. The world must be made safe for democracy. Its peace must be planted upon the tested foundations of political liberty...."

This is directly opposed to the principle of handing over areas predominantly German or Ukrainian to the Poles. Lloyd George opposed the idea of handing over so many Germans to the Poles, pointing out that the Poles had a different religion, and that they had never proved in history that they were capable of ruling themselves. He expressed the view that such an action would sooner or later lead to a new war in East Europe. Woodrow Wilson, on the other hand, abandoned his principle of self-determination, and once remarked that he was for the Poles and against the Germans when there was anything to decide upon. No one has, apparently, ever troubled about the rights of self-determination in Poland since then. The minorities have fought alone - a losing fight against the Poles.

8

Dreams of Empire

The Poles say that they are the outposts of Europe, and once saved civilisation from Asiatic hordes. Now in their own Polish areas the Poles did build up a State which was excellent in many respects, but which failed to survive as a result of internal strife. The nobles constantly fought against each other, and did not unite until they found themselves under the domination of Czarist Russia. The Russians treated the Poles badly, and it was a good thing when the Poles regained their independence. Unluckily for all concerned, however, the Poles were also given non-Polish districts, and they, in their turn, have ruled over their own minorities badly.

History should have taught us better, for the Ukrainians had once before lived under Polish rule - and it was then that the Asiatic hordes, under Jenghiz Khan, were first defeated. Only there is a slight error here. It was the Ukrainian people and their volunteer guards, the Cossacks, who saved Europe from the Mongols, and not the Poles. As, however, Poland claimed sovereignty over Ukraine at the time, many Poles do, no doubt, genuinely believe it was their ancestors who fought. But that is a mistake.

The Ukraine was formerly known as the Grand Duchy of Kiev and was the first Slav country to make its mark in history. In the 11th and 12th centuries Kiev was at the height of its power, but later internal strife and dynastic quarrels weakened the nation. As a result, Jenghiz Khan and his hordes found them an easy prey - or, at least, a comparatively easy one. The Ukrainians made an effort to unite, and resisted the attack made at the beginning of the 13th century. In 1224 the army of the Grand Duchy of Kiev was routed, but guerrilla warfare continued with such desperation that it was not until 16 years later that the Asiatics succeeded in capturing and destroying the capital. After this, the guerrilla war did not entirely cease, but the power of the Ukrainians was broken. They have never been entirely independent since, but have never lost their dream of independence. I am personally acquainted with many Ukrainians, most of them exiles, and they all hope and believe that their nation will again become independent and powerful. They are mainly to be found in Russia, while some are included in Rumania, but they also form Poland's greatest minority. Their language is distinct from all others. Several Ukrainian newspapers appear in Canada and U.S.A.

The Ukrainians were next under the control of Lithuania, then a powerful State, but in 1569 the Poles obtained control of the whole of Lithuania, including the Ukraine. This was the origin of the Polish claim to part of the Ukraine, granted them at Versailles, and to Vilna, which they seized against the wishes of the Allies.

One of the worst chapters in European history followed. Ukrainians were ruthlessly massacred on occasion; they were robbed of the last vestige of semi-independence. Even their religion was forbidden them, and they were ordered to leave the Orthodox Church for the Church of Rome. Polish was introduced as the only permissible language.

In the towns the Polish policy was fairly successful. Rich Ukrainians - outwardly at least - came to terms in order to retain their worldly goods, but the main body of the people, engaged in agriculture, hunting and fishing, rejected all Polish measures whether peaceable or forcible. Many of them were killed, but in those days it was comparatively easy for groups of people to escape the Polish punitive expeditions. Serfdom, however, was widely introduced. The Ukrainians answered by attacking Poles and "converts", i.e. Ukrainians who submitted to the Poles, on sight. A period of lawlessness followed. The Poles were brutal in their methods, but their control was mainly confined to the Western Ukraine. Eastwards, on the other hand, raiding parties of Tartars harassed the Ukrainians, and here they were compelled to form volunteer forces for defence.

The Tartars might have overrun wide areas of Europe had it not been for the Ukrainians, to whom we owe a great debt of gratitude. Ukrainian Cossacks kept the raiders at bay, and finally a Cossack Republic was established. A leader was elected, to hold supreme power in time of war. The Ukrainians welcomed the establishment of this republic, which though not entirely independent, made certain agreements with other countries. The power of the Cossacks only extended to the South-Eastern parts of the Ukraine. In the other parts, meantime, the struggle went on, religious persecution being the main cause, for the Ukrainians cling to their Orthodox faith.

Little notice was taken by the world at large of these gallant struggles carried on by the Ukrainians, though Oliver Cromwell felt a good deal of sympathy for the brave people. He once referred to his contemporary, the Ukrainian statesman Bohdan Chmelnyckyj, as the uncrowned king of the Ukraine. Later the Poles conquered again, and when, afterwards, Russia seized both the Ukraine and Poland, both nations became fellow-sufferers so to speak.

This makes the present position all the harder to understand. Poles and Ukrainians went side by side in chains to Siberia in pre-War days in the cause of their independence; but when, after the War, the Poles gained their independence and, at the same time, control over a part of the Ukraine, they applied the same methods as of yore. The Ukrainians were forgotten at Versailles, although they were represented there.

In Warsaw, Poles told me that they had a powerful army and were united. Perhaps the Poles themselves are, but the inhabitants of Poland as a whole are definitely not united. It would be a mistake to believe that the Ukrainians, White Russians, Jews and Germans, the Lithuanians and the Slovaks in Poland are united to those who oppress them. The

Ukrainians and Germans are only longing to escape. The Poles are not really united either, for the poor among them are very dissatisfied. I have seen hundreds of men and women sleeping in the open in meadows adjoining the Vistula. Beggars in rags approached me as I walked along the streets of Lemberg; dozens of hotel touts tried to persuade me to visit their hotels in Warsaw. Sitting on the terrace of one of Cracow's biggest cafes, adjoining the park, I was accosted by dozens of beggars, including many children, who stopped in front of my table to ask for alms. One small boy, thin and poorly clad, begged for bits of bread and lumps of sugar, which he took away in a dirty, torn bag.

The workers earn about 150 zloty per month on an average, or some six pounds. That amounts to precisely 28 shillings per week in a month of 30 days. Few civil servants earn more than about double this sum, even in Warsaw. But rents are high. I saw small self-contained flats in Warsaw fetching more than the average flat would in Maida Vale. Even the most simple flats (all Warsaw lives in flats) are expensive in proportion to the family income. Quite often, half the earnings will be spent on rent. Taxes and insurance contributions are high, and are deducted from the wages and salaries.

It is quite a mistake to suppose that 28 shillings will buy more in Poland than in England. True, if one moved from Mayfair to Posen, the latter would appear to be cheap; one must compare the West End of London with the fashionable quarter of Warsaw. Comparing the cost of living in English and Polish towns and villages generally, we find that a shilling buys at least as much in England as in Poland, while our workers pay no taxes on small wages as the Poles do. In the country, of course, wages are even lower and, as in England, prices are not so high as in the towns. Poverty in Poland is widespread, especially in the South-East. First-class hotel charges are on the general European scale.

All the minorities are subjected to certain restrictions. They have schools of their own, which they run themselves, but the Poles constantly find fault with their management, closing them down under one pretext or other. Their newspapers are also banned from time to time.

The seizing of newspapers is not confined to the journals of the minorities, however, and I repeatedly saw Polish papers seized. Policemen stroll about until they see a newsboy, and then look through his papers. The newsboy stands aside with a broad smile on his lips. The seized papers are counted and the policeman gives the newsvendor a receipt. No crowd collects. One becomes accustomed to such things. One can imagine what excitement there would be if the police seized papers in London and strolled around with their arms full of dailies. In Warsaw it is quite commonplace.

The Polish Press is not united in support of the idea of an alliance with Moscow, and not all Poles agree with it. In fact it is not so long since the *Gazeta Polska,* one of the leading dailies, stated (12. 11. 1937) that "the population of Danzig is German by a vast majority.... No one can contradict this." I met Poles who did contradict it, claiming that Danzig really had a Polish population. Needless to say, none of them had ever been there. Those who had, admitted that the people were German, but declared that the town was "historically Polish."

Though the Poles are not all of the same opinion, many of them have unfortunately misunderstood things, and believe that England is willing to help them "regain" wide areas in Central Europe. I well remember when the Labour Party protested loudly against the Polish attack on Russia in 1920. It is true that the Russians afterwards threatened to occupy the whole of Poland, but it was the Poles who began it. In 1921 the attack on Lithuania, and the seizure of Vilna, took place, In the same year the Poles attacked Upper Silesia, against all the peace terms. In 1930 the Ukraine was pacified with a brutality fortunately seldom known in our days. In 1938 the Poles annexed a corner of Czecho-Slovakia, including parts with a German majority and one district that was mainly populated by Slovaks. At present the Danzigers are wondering if they will come next. And during all this time, hundreds of thousands of Germans have been forced to emigrate by the Polish terror.

One might ask why particularly the Germans, and not, say, the Ukrainians, should have emigrated if they are both persecuted. The answer is, of course, that whilst the Germans have crossed the frontier to the Reich, the Ukrainians have no country of their own. Incidentally, the Poles have tried particularly hard to drive the Germans out of Upper Silesia, due to the fact that the area is industrialised and hence thickly populated. In the Corridor, the building of Gdynia as a port has enabled Poles to settle there, but as there is little scope in Upper Silesia, the only way to make more room is to force the Germans to emigrate if possible. (It may be safely assumed that hundreds of thousands of people do not leave their homes *en masse* without some very good reason, and, as already mentioned, the Poles themselves admit that the Germans have left in large numbers.)

Very naturally their fellow-countrymen across the frontier feel indignant, and it is not probable that the Russians are pleased with Poland, either. After all, a big White Russian minority still exists in Poland and some Russians consider the idea of an Anschluss to be good.

There seems no good reason to believe that in the event of war the Russians would really assist the Poles to any great extent. General Sikorski, writing in the *Svenska Dagbladet* (April 5th, 1939), expressed the opinion that benevolent neutrality was all that could be expected of Russia, and he expressly added that the most which could possibly be given (the maximum help, he called it) would be the assistance of the Russian Air Force. "Any further aid," he went on, "is not desired," the reason given being that the States bordering U.S.S.R. do not want "to expose themselves to the danger of being overrun by the Bolsheviks." Another sentence in the General's article was that "the situation would have to be really desperate, and Poland completely overrun by an enemy, before the acceptance of Russian help could be considered."

This attitude of the Poles is hardly surprising. At present, visitors from abroad are not admitted until they have paid 25 zloty for a visa, and even then the control is so strict that actually the number of the hotel bedroom occupied by a guest is included in the details to be given immediately on arrival to the police. I have never heard of any other country going to these extremes. But it is easy to understand that a people with such an attitude towards foreigners is not likely to welcome the idea of admitting hundreds of thousands of Russians in their midst.

The Poles do not wish anyone to occupy their country. On the contrary, they are anxious to occupy areas outside their own present borders.

It is interesting to note that Poland once considered the Corridor to be worthless if she could not also have East Prussia, an idea never completely abandoned. Roman Dmowski, in his memorandum to President Wilson, dated October 8th, 1918, clearly pointed this out. He remarked that if East Prussia were to remain German territory, the Corridor should also be retained. The Corridor, he went on, was of no value to Poland without East Prussia, for it would never cease to be a bone of contention between Poland and Germany. Germany would always hanker after a linking bridge at the expense of Poland.

A prominent Pole recently suggested to me that the solution for Germany, if she did not like the idea of having an isolated province, was to exchange East Prussia for the Corridor. As East Prussia is 100% German, this proposal would hardly lead to a settlement, but it was proposed to me in all seriousness.

When the Corridor was established, Sforza said that "no serious politician had believed in the long existence of the Corridor emergency solution." In a book written afterwards, Sforza made the following statement:

> "These Poles were terribly logical and obstinate with the result that everyone felt troubled about their perpetual claims. If they were to be believed, half Europe was once Polish and should have become Polish again. Thus it came about, for example, that diplomatic Europe, when Dmowski demanded the cession of East Prussia to Poland, in order, as he logically said, to avoid the contradiction of the Danzig Corridor, was so embittered that, if only Lloyd George had had his way, we might perhaps have experienced a fourth division of Poland in the end."

Dmowski angrily accused Lloyd George of playing into the hands of the Germans, and made this remarkable statement in his memoirs:

> "If it had not been for Lloyd George, our Western frontiers would have been very different. Only a man who was under a direct obligation to the Germans or the Jews would protect the interests of the Germans with such zeal.
>
> "The work of destroying the findings of the Territorial Commission began with less important matters, and then passed on to more ponderous affairs. First of all he prevented the four German districts near Marienburg from being handed to Poland, then he saw that a plebiscite was held. In the Danzig question, too, he was victorious in the struggle against Wilson and Clemenceau and the 'Free State' was finally agreed upon."

Incidentally, Tomasini called the Polish Corridor an "incurable wound in Germany's flesh," and it was only owing to Clemenceau's urgency that this area was ever given to Poland at all. I well remember how everyone in London was against it at the time. Woodrow Wilson was not pleased about it either, for, as he pointed out to R. St. Baker in April, 1919, France's only real interest in Poland was to weaken Germany by giving the Poles areas to which they had no claim. The Poles have always considered that the Corridor question was bound to lead to a war, but to a war which would widen their own frontiers. There have been dozens of clear, unmistakable statements to that effect in various publications, and I select the following from the *Mocarstwowiec* because it appeared in 1930, i.e. before Hitler became Chancellor:

> "We are aware that war between Poland and Germany cannot be avoided. We must systematically and energetically prepare ourselves for this war. The present generation will see that a new victory at Grunwald will be inscribed in the pages of history. But

we shall fight this Grunwald in the suburbs of Berlin. Our ideal is to round Poland off with frontiers on the Oder in the West and the Neisse in Lausatia, and to reincorporate Prussia, from the Pregel to the Spree. In this war no prisoners will be taken, there will be no room for humanitarian feelings. We shall surprise the whole world in our war with Germany."

Such boasts and threats as these have not, of course, been made by the whole Polish people. On the contrary, the ordinary man in the street in Poland definitely opposes the idea of fighting for a new frontier and is all for peace. But there is an element in Poland which demands that Germany should be partitioned. A bank clerk when I changed a five-pound note in a small Polish town, asked me if I knew that there was a suburb called Nowawes in Berlin, adding that the "Nazis were changing its name to hide the fact that it was really Polish!" A hotel porter in a larger town told me that Wannsee, Berlin's bathing beach, was once Polish, and that the Berliners thus sunned themselves on true Polish soil. I heard many other similar claims, all absurd, and most of them contradictory.

9

The Poles at home

The Poles have an exaggerated idea of their own importance. It was this in part which led to the extended frontiers which the Labour Party used to attack so strongly. *The Labour Speakers' Handbook* (1922-3) remarked under the heading "Poland" that "in the newly constituted State of Poland a large non-Polish population has been included. Exact statements on the whole of this cannot be given because the frontiers of Poland have not been finally fixed.... Nearly all West Prussia has been annexed to Poland, although two-thirds of the people are German and all the civilisation of the country has been due to Germany. A plebiscite was not allowed; if it had been, it would have gone overwhelmingly in favour of Germany.... The whole of the province of Posen has been annexed to Poland, although in the Western part there is a German majority.... The policy of Labour is to rectify these unjust territorial arrangements...."

A further example of their arrogance is to be found in the National Anthem. I would not by any means say that the text of national anthems is typical of the feelings of the people who sing it, but still it may be of interest to quote the words of Verse II, which are as follows:

> Crossing the Vistula, crossing the Warta,
> We shall be true Poles;
> We learned a lesson from Buonaparte

How to conquer everything.

That is hardly the spirit of a nation, desiring nothing more than to be left in peace. To "conquer everything" (which might also be rendered "to conquer all") may be a figure of speech, but the direct reference to Buonaparte leaves no doubt that the Poles think in terms of wide conquests. The Polish text of the last two lines is:

Dal nam przykl ad Bonaparte
Jak zwyciezac mamy.

That is not just a joke. The Poles actually did fight side by side with Napoleon for the conquest of Europe, against England, Prussia and other countries. It was not, as in so many other cases, that Napoleon placed one of his own relations on the throne and then claimed the country as his ally. Prince Joseph Poniatowski, nephew of the last king of Poland, fought for him, and fell at the Battle of Leipzig. His statue, which is the object of pilgrimages to-day, stands in Warsaw, in front of the Polish tomb of the Unknown Warrior. I saw his burial place next to that of Kosciusko in a vault of the Wawel in Cracow. Napoleon is much revered as an example of what a man should be; after all, he established the Duchy of Warsaw in 1807.

But when Napoleon was defeated by Wellington and Blücher, Poland's dream ended. The Congress of Vienna awarded most of Poland to Russia - who had also suffered under the joint attack of the French and Poles, and had been forced to burn Moscow in 1812 to avoid a French occupation, it will be remembered.

The Russians did not trouble themselves unduly about the terms under which Poland was entrusted to them. The Allies of 1815 (including the Prussians, though not the French) hoped that Russia would give all due consideration to the Polish rights, including self-government. 104 years later, the Allies (this time including the French, but not the Prussians) entrusted other minorities to Poland - and with no better results. Self-government was also promised - but never came into effect. So does history repeat itself.

Poland has had several great leaders, but they have always failed in the hour of victory by oppressing their beaten enemies, and by pushing their demands too far, or by quarrelling among themselves on some question of dynasty.

The late Marshal Pilsudski was a brilliant exception. He is to-day a national hero in Poland. I climbed the hill on which a great plaque is erected to his memory outside Cracow, to be followed by a monument. To many of the pilgrims to this hill only Pilsudski's military ability is remembered. His statesmanship, at least as great, is mostly forgotten.

Joseph Pilsudski was born at Zulów in Vilna; his heart was buried at Vilna at the foot of his mother's grave, at his own request. He was born on December 5th, 1867. He studied at the University of Kharkoff, wishing to become a doctor; but he took more interest in liberating Poland than in medicine, and it was not long before he was being sent in chains to Siberia. From 1887 to 1892 he suffered exile, then returned to Warsaw, where he founded the Polish Socialist Party, which had for its aim the independence of Poland. Pilsudski started a paper which the police promptly banned, he was arrested and imprisoned in the Warsaw Citadel, afterwards being transferred to St. Petersburg. There, in the X Pavillion, he suffered solitary confinement in cell No. 31. On May 13th, 1901, he escaped and went to Cracow (then Austria). In 1906 and 1907 he organised Polish volunteers for the struggle against Russia. He started an organisation of Polish Riflemen in 1910 - not with the object of attacking Austria or Germany, where the Poles were reasonably well treated, but in order to attack Russia at the first opportunity.

That opportunity came when the Great War broke out. On August 6th, 1914, Pilsudski and his riflemen left Cracow with the Polish flag at their head to fight side by side with the Central Powers. After the Russian defeat, Pilsudski had some disagreement with the Germans, who imprisoned him at Magdeburg, but he was afterwards released. He was then nominated First Marshal of Poland, after having occupied the post of "Chief of State." In 1922 he retired from public life, somewhat disillusioned, it is said. But in 1926 Poland was on the verge of a new partition, and Pilsudski took over control, despite the Government. In fact, he had first to overcome Polish opposition of a very definite character.

He had in the meanwhile studied politics, and now proved one of the greatest statesmen Poland ever had. In 1934 he made an agreement with Hitler when hardly anyone imagined that such a thing was possible. A lesser man would not have accomplished this. Hitler deserves equal praise in this respect, but then his country was the stronger. Pilsudski, in a weaker position secured a fair agreement for his country, which is the essence of true statesmanship. His body is preserved in the crypt of the Wawel Cathedral in Cracow.

The memory of Pilsudski is still alive in Poland, but his statesmanship, alas, is forgotten. He is remembered only as the warrior and victor. A prominent Pole told me that if Pilsudski had lived he would have attacked Germany and prevented all danger. I suggested that if he had been alive he would have assured a long peace by agreement with his neighbour, as he did in 1934. My friend was struck by the idea, which had obviously never occurred to him before. After a slight pause he said, "Perhaps you are right!"

Colonel Beck, the Foreign Minister, is one of the best known Poles of the present time. He was formerly a staunch follower of Pilsudski, but has since changed his political views. He undoubtedly acts as he thinks best for his country, but unfortunately he lacks the far-sightedness of the late Marshal Pilsudski.

General Rydz was chosen by Pilsudski as his successor in leading the nation, and when the Marshal died his wish was respected. He was born in 1886, and was very serious as a boy. I was told that he organised a schoolboy campaign against smoking when only eleven years old. His parents died in his early childhood. Rydz is a man of great ability, but he is a dreamer. At school his main talents were in drawing and painting, while he steeped himself in history. His special hero has always been

Napoleon, as is openly admitted in Warsaw to-day. He has stated, by the way, that Pilsudski's arrest in Germany after Russia's defeat was due to the Marshal's refusal to organise a Polish army to assist the Germans. Rydz was nominated General by Pilsudski himself. The dream of Napoleonic greatness now not only influences the head of the army, but also many of its senior officers.

Pilsudski was perhaps the first Pole to learn the lesson of give and take. No less a person than Pitt found that it was hard to come to a settlement with Poland. He advised the Poles at the end of the 18th century to leave Danzig to Prussia, and Thorn was also to be ceded. The Polish Parliament refused. Pitt persisted, however, and told the Polish ambassador in Holland that these two towns should go to Prussia in December 1790. Prussia proved more pliable, although the stronger, and abandoned the claim to Thorn in the interests of peace, while through Pitt's good offices a big reduction on shipping dues on the Vistula was assured Poland. This excellent example from the pages of history, of a British Statesman securing an agreement between Prussia and Poland when things seemed hopeless, and Poland was already claiming Danzig, should prove a precedent for the present case.

10

The influence of Napoleon

I have shown how the Poles admired Napoleon. But history shows that the French did not share this feeling. On the contrary, they wrote things which, if true, make terrible accusations - and it would be hard to believe they were inventions.

A typical example is to be found in the Memoirs of one of the best and most upright officers in Napoleon's army. It has a Napoleonic stamp, for the petit caporal left this officer instructions in his will to complete the Memoirs. This writer, General Baron de Marbot, who participated in all the big campaigns, wrote as follows in Volume III (*The retreat from Russia*):

> "...The desire to enrich themselves gave us a new enemy from the ranks of our own allies, the Poles. The Marshal of Saxony, son of one of their kings, rightly said, 'The Poles are the greatest robbers on earth, not even respecting the property of their own fathers.'
>
> "...On the march and in camp, they stole whatever they saw. But as finally no more trust was placed in them and individual acts of theft became very difficult, they decided to operate on a big scale. For this purpose they organised bands, doffed their helmets, and put on peasants' caps, crept out of the camp, and met

at a pre-arranged point when it became dark, then attacking their own camp while uttering the war-cry of the Cossacks. The false Cossacks returned after the work of plundering was completed, and were to be found in the ranks of the French army the next morning, only to become 'Cossacks' again on the next night.

"Several generals and colonels decided to punish these disgraceful thefts. One night, 50 Poles were taken by surprise as they attacked the camp as Cossacks... and shot...."

The translation is made from the original French. But more than a century later, the French placed no greater confidence in their Polish friends. In 1929, for example, Pierre Valmigère wrote, in an article entitled "France, Allemagne et Pologne":

"Do you believe in the gratitude of the Poles? - It is obviously not in the interests of France to support Poland at present, though this is done from reasons of stupid sentimentality. She (France) believes she loves Poland, but she does not know this nation, which had hardly regained its independence when everything within reach was grabbed into its clutches; which has more than 40 per cent. of non-Polish citizens who hate her, secretly in revolt and only awaiting an opportunity to free themselves.

"Does France know that this Poland is not even satisfied with its 40 per cent. population of foreign origin, but that it carries the madness and expansion mania to such limits that it demands Silesia from Beuthen to Oppeln, the whole of the Ukraine, Danzig and East Prussia?"

At Versailles, when Danzig was to have been handed entirely to the tender mercies of Poland, Lloyd George said that injustice in a moment of triumph would never be forgotten or forgiven, for which reason he was against placing more Germans than necessary under foreign rule. Lloyd George also stated in so many words that the Poles had never proved that they could rule even themselves, and that the proposal of the Polish Commission would, in his opinion, lead to war sooner or later.

It was not until Marshal Pilsudski ruled in Poland that these wild ideas of a vast Empire were temporarily abandoned in Warsaw. Pilsudski was a passionately patriotic Pole, but precisely for this reason he determined to avoid struggles with his neighbours which could only be to the detriment of his own country. That was the best proof of his greatness. Pilsudski was certainly aware that the Treaty of Versailles had treated Germany unfairly, and given Poland more land than she was historically or ethnographically entitled to. But he was a Pole and represented the interests of his own people. He realised the great importance of peace with Germany, and accepted the Non-Aggression Pact, which was to last ten years. Poland needed peace for reconstruction, just as Germany did. One condition of this Pact was that Germans in Poland and Poles in Germany were to be well treated. The Poles in Germany are small in number, and there has been little friction between them and the Reich, but the Germans in Poland are a huge minority, and there had continually been disagreements from 1919 onwards. Pilsudski and Hitler came to an agreement. Pilsudski was heart and soul for this Pact, but there was a powerful group in Poland which was bitterly opposed to friendship with the Germans, and which waited for the first opportunity to turn the helm. After Pilsudski's death, the attempt to turn the Germans into 100% Poles was resumed.

This was bound to cause tension. Had Pilsudski lived, an agreement would probably have been unnecessary, for the Pact would have continued. And if a new agreement had been needed, the Polish Marshal would certainly have secured one which was just to all, and assured the interests of the Poles as well. Unfortunately the Poles to-day have been persuaded by their journalists and politicians that Pilsudski aimed at making all the Eastern half of Europe Polish - which was by no means the case. It was a sad day for Poland's true interests when this great man passed away before a lasting settlement to all questions had been reached. For the German-Polish Pact did not settle points under dispute, nor did it aim at doing so. The Pact was a kind of armistice to last ten years, during which time all questions were to be looked into, and if possible settled, by a round-table conference between representatives of Berlin and Warsaw. This showed the true greatness of the agreement. Neither Poland nor Germany saw eye to eye with the other, but Pilsudski and Hitler signed a pact despite disagreements. Many minor points were settled after the Pact came into effect, but the main questions were left for the future - and Pilsudski's death prevented the new friendship between the two countries from maturing. This raises the question as to how it comes about that there are so many Germans in Poland. For the German inhabitants are not only to be found in the provinces allotted to Poland unjustly in 1919. They are spread throughout the country - in the Polish parts as a minority, of course, but in the Corridor and Upper Silesia as the majority.

When the first really Polish State was established by the Viking Prince, sometimes called Dago, and otherwise known as Misika, the new country was under German sovereignty. And thus the Polish dukes and nobles visited the German Courts, keeping in close touch with Western progress, such as it was in those days. These nobles invited German knights and monks to come to Poland, and many did so, where they established religious and educational centres. The first Gothic buildings in Poland, some of which still stand, owe their origin to these early German settlers.

German merchants and craftsmen followed, and as early as the 12th century they were sprinkled among the Slav population. The first towns already existed, though of course few in number, and it was only in the 13th century that they became numerous. Most of these towns had only German inhabitants, the Poles being ineligible to become citizens, and the German language and customs were maintained for centuries, for the Poles showed little aptitude or inclination for city life, even when this was open to them, which was at a slightly later date. Many towns differed little from the mediaeval towns in Germany itself, examples being Cracow, Posen, Kalish, Lublin and Peisern. Many of the towns founded in Poland had German names from the start. Examples are Lemberg, Landshut, Neumarkt, Liebwarte, Landskrone, Timberg and Frawenstat. Some of the German towns, and particularly Cracow, were so powerful that they often played a decisive part in the dynastic struggles between the Polish dukes. Forts usually guarded the towns. A glance at the splendid walls of Cracow, still in a fine state of preservation, easily enables one to realise the strategic power that such a town could exercise in those times of comparatively primitive weapons.

In the course of time German peasants also settled in the sparsely populated country areas. There were actually large enclaves, such as that which still existed at the beginning of the 18th century at the foot of the Carpathians. Many of these Germans gradually learned to speak Polish, and are now regarded as Poles. But in numerous cases their surnames remind one of their origin. The Christian names are Polish, however. In Posen and West Galicia German settlements were gradually established on a fairly large scale. Now these Germans were free men, while the Poles still lived in a state of serfdom, so that the Germans had more scope to make progress. Hundreds of German villages came into being. The Polish peasants, as they gained more liberty, adopted many customs of the Germans. **Absolute proof of the fact that the Germans were in many areas before the Poles is to be found in the registers in old buildings, where the very earliest entries are in German. This is the case in innumerable towns. The oldest municipal register at Thorn does not contain a single word of Polish, it is all in German. The oldest municipal register in Cracow begins in German.** Early council deliberations at Thorn, Posen, Cracow and many other towns took place in German only. *[Emphasis added by The Scriptorium.]*

The German character of many old buildings has already been remarked on. Some of these were German-built, while others were merely based on German style. The St. Mary's Church at Cracow was built by Wernher and Heinrich Parler, who hailed from Gmünd in Swabia. Sermons there were delivered in German until 1537. The altar was carved by the German, Veit Stoss. The old Cloth Halls in the Cracow market place, which rank high among the sights of Europe, were built by another German, Jakob Lindentolde. Even the Wawel Castle thanks its existence very largely to Germans, one of whom, Hans Boner, was responsible for the financing, its construction and, to some extent, for its artistic excellence. The Cathedral at Lemberg is the work of a German architect, Peter Stecher; St. John's Church at Thorn was built by another German, Johann Gotland. In Warsaw, there are several German buildings, including the old Gothic Cathedral of St. John's.

The swampy areas adjoining the Vistula and Warta were reclaimed by Germans at a time when the Poles were still serfs. At the close of the 18th century German settlements extended to Lodz.

Large German villages sprang up, and existed in their original form for many generations. They form the nucleus of many a present village. The names of such villages include Königshuld, Luisenfeld and Friedrichshagen, after the Prussian Royal Family, and various names reminding the settlers of the homes of their forefathers, such as Neu-Württemberg, Leonberg, Effingshausen, Erdmannsweiler, Hochweiler, Neu-Sulzfeld, Neu-Ilvesheim, and the like. These names were afterwards officially translated into Polish but some still live in the hearts of the people. In 1885 there were roughly a thousand German villages in so-called Congress Poland alone, and this number was on the increase. At the beginning of the 19th century new settlements were established, mainly by weavers from Lower Silesia, Saxony, Thuringia and the Sudetenland. There were about 30,000 such settlers, including women and children. A further 20,000 cloth-makers made their homes in Congress Poland about the same time.

Many of the great men of Poland were of German origin, including Copernicus and the philosopher Hoene. The names of General Haller and Colonel Beck actually sound German.

I quote the above to show how the Germans came to appear in distant parts of Poland, and what they did there. There can be no question of handing over German villages in Central Poland on this account, but it is clear that the Germans have assisted in building Polish towns and cities, in developing industry, and in improving things generally. Past co-operation between Germans and Poles should be regarded as a stepping-stone to future agreement and neighbourly relations. The Russians were the traditional enemies of the Poles, not the Germans.

The Polish Prince Radziwill adopted this view when, during the Great War, he asserted that "the common enemy of Poland and Germany is Russia. The final aim of the war is the same for both Poland and Germany. History proves this. Let us look at a sketch of the history of Poland, and we shall see that Poland has always regarded the Muscovite realm as her worst enemy. There can be no doubt about this. There has been no comparatively lengthy period without a war, more recently without a rising, against the Muscovites.... All these risings were against Russia only, including the last revolution in 1905...." Then again: "We Poles know that Posen is a part of Prussia, and always will be, and we do not dream of cutting a part out of the body of the country which liberates us."

Despite Prince Radziwill's words, Posen might better be left to Poland, so as to avoid any serious disputes. But the words of this prominent Pole are nevertheless of interest.

Many far-seeing Poles were against the inclusion of non-Polish territory in their State, and with good reason, for a people who number 20 millions can hardly digest a minority 75% as large as themselves - or, rather, a group of minorities. The way in which the present Polish frontier was fixed has been partly described in the *Kurjer Poznansky* by Dr. Rydlewski, a member of the Polish Commission in Paris. He showed the difficulties which Marshal Pilsudski's representative, Dr. Dluski, and Professor Nitsch, of Cracow, placed in the way of the two heads of the Commission, Dmowski and Paderewski, during the negotiations at Versailles.

His description is extremely illuminating. "During my stay in Paris," he writes, "I received an invitation to a session of the Polish Commission. In reply to the question as to where I thought the frontier in the Posen area should be, I declared briefly that I demanded the whole of the Grand Duchy of Posen without any cuts. Professor Nitsch of Cracow protested with energy and determination. He stated that he had toured the whole area as a philologist, and had found that the Western part of this area was unquestionably German. 'I did not find a single Polish town or Polish village,' Professor Nitsch assured us, 'and I did not hear a single word of Polish in these regions.' 'Why,' exclaimed Professor Nitsch, greatly moved, 'perhaps you want to take Bomst, Bentschen, Birnbaum and Meseritz away from the Germans?' 'Of course,' I replied, 'these districts and towns belong to us!'"

Dr. Rydlewski went on to remark in the course of the same article that Professor Nitsch's attitude had troubled him, and a discussion followed, when the Professor declared the areas under discussion were all German. Dr. Dluski then joined in with protests against the proposed annexation of Posen and, according to Dr. Rydlewski, asked the latter ironically if he did not wish to annex Berlin as well.

Dmowski afterwards grumbled about Marshal Pilsudski's "difficult attitude," declaring that the Marshal was not very anxious to have Prussian areas, and that he also wished to give the Ukrainians a part of East Galicia. Pilsudski wanted a Polish State, and he no longer cherished the earlier dreams of an Empire. He saw that foreign areas were not worth having. It is clear that Pilsudski would never have been willing to risk the independence of his people in a war to retain non-Polish land.

11

Famous men quoted

There was a tendency at one time to describe the Polish Corridor in brief but pithy phrases. General Weygand called it "useless in peace, and not to be defended in war." M. Herbette, formerly French Ambassador at Moscow, said in an interview with the *Zürcher Zeitung* that the "return of the Polish Corridor is inevitable."

The Corridor has been criticised by numerous prominent Englishmen at various times. Lord Dickinson, an expert on minority questions, thought that no one could travel in East Prussia or Danzig without coming to the conclusion that the present state could not go on. Lord Rothermere described the division of Germany by the Corridor as the worst part of the whole Peace Treaty and referred to the Corridor as a provocation for Germany and a danger for England. Professor Dawson, one of Lloyd George's collaborators, and expert in German-Polish frontier questions, stated that the Poles did not need the Corridor. Mr. Garvin, Editor of the *Observer*, declared that England would not go to war for the Corridor. Lord d'Abernon regarded the Corridor as the chief danger in Europe after the danger on the Franco-German frontier had diminished. Sir Robert Donald, formerly Editor of the *News Chronicle*, considered the Corridor to be a threatening area.

Americans have held the same views. Senator Borah stated in an interview that a revision of the frontier of Upper Silesia and the Corridor was necessary. Senator Johnson, in the New York *Sun*, said that Wilson had told him that three things had disappointed him, and that one was the handing over to Poland of German areas. Colonel Powell described the Corridor as a powder-barrel left by Wilson.

Dozens of other similar statements might be added, but no purpose could be served by printing pages of such quotations, which all amount to the same thing. Lloyd George, Signor Nitti, Senator Borah, Marshal Foch, General Weygand, Ambassador Herbette, Lord Rothermere, Lord Dickinson, Mr. Garvin and Senator Johnson were only a few of the many authorities who adopted the same point of view, i.e. that the Corridor was a danger that would have to be dealt with sooner or later.

The Polish Ambassador, M. Filipowicz, once tried to persuade Senator Borah that the Corridor was Polish, and the Senator ironically remarked that there would certainly soon be 100 per cent. Poles in the Corridor if Poland continued her present policy.

The really astonishing thing is that the Corridor was ever decided upon as an emergency solution at all. And just why it was considered necessary to find an emergency solution is not clear. President Wilson opposed the idea, at least until the end of 1918, as being against the principle of self-determination, and in October of that year he asked Paderewski and Dmowski if a free harbour would not meet their needs. But the view that the national rights must be respected did not begin with Wilson. Throughout the War, British Ministers said they would stand by it. The first of them was the late Earl of Oxford and Asquith (then Mr. Asquith), who, as Premier, stated in the House of Commons on August 6th, 1914, two days after the outbreak of hostilities, that Britain was fighting for two things. The second, in Asquith's own words, was "to vindicate the principle - which in these days when force, material force, sometimes seems to be the dominant influence and factor in the development of mankind - we are fighting to vindicate the principle that small nationalities are not to be crushed in defiance of international good faith by the arbitrary will of a strong and overmastering Power."

But the principle mentioned, that small nationalities should not be crushed, was clearly forgotten in 1919. President Wilson on April 2nd, 1917, asserted that "we are but one of the champions of the rights of mankind. We shall be satisfied when those rights have been made as secure as the faith and the freedom of nations can make them. Just because we fight without rancour and without selfish object, seeking nothing for ourselves but what we shall wish to share with all free peoples, we shall, I feel confident, conduct our operations as belligerents without passion and ourselves observe with proud punctilio the principles of right and of fair play we profess to be fighting for...."

There can be no doubt but that these words were spoken in all earnestness, and represented the view of the speakers at the time they were used; but by 1919 all this was forgotten. Who referred to "the principles of right and of fair play" when it came to satisfying the various insatiable delegations who all demanded slices of Germany?

I have remarked that if Danzig shall become German again, as it wishes to, this is merely the fulfilment of the words of Asquith, Lloyd George and Wilson, who favoured self-determination. Wilson said on February 11th, 1918, that nationalities and land must not be treated *as though* they were pawns in a game. All the speeches of British and American statesmen made during the War, of which I have quoted two characteristic examples (Asquith and Wilson) verbatim above, were against regarding groups of people or plots of land as chess-men. The Danzigers became figures in a game of chess in spite of that: the Polish Corridor was another pawn in the game.

Upper Silesia was a third. The Allies said it should be left to Germany, but the Poles immediately checkmated.

It is impossible for any fair-minded person to deny that Wilson's Fourteen Points did not permit such German areas to be placed under the control of other Powers.

And if we consider the Ukrainians, we find that the same applies. No nationality was to become a pawn in the game; fair play was to be assured; America, according to Wilson, was "but one of the champions of the rights of mankind."

The Ukrainians were divided between Russia, Poland, Czecho-Slovakia and Rumania by the peace treaties. We cannot excuse ourselves by saying we had a quarrel with them. Neither England nor America has ever had a quarrel with the Ukrainians in the whole of their history. We cannot claim that the Ukraine was split up in the interests of the balance of power, for these people would have helped to establish such a balance. If we had created an independent Ukrainian State, we should have earned their gratitude and had a friend with a population of 45 millions in Europe. The rights of small nationalities were simply ignored at Versailles and Trianon. The case of the Ukrainians proves this clearly enough.

The least we can do even now is to assure them their own local government. Or should we fight for the Poles in order that they may prevent the Ukrainians from teaching their children their own language?

We must, in accordance with war pledges, do our best to see that each nationality enjoys all possible independence. This includes the Poles. But why only the Poles? Why not the Ukrainians as well?

Twenty years have passed without anything being done for the minorities, who cannot be expected to wait another score or two of years. There is proverbially no time like the present. What we are prepared to do for Poland we should also be willing to do for Danzig, the Corridor, Upper Silesia and the Ukraine, i.e. to use our influence to gain each of these areas a maximum of liberty.

It was Clemenceau who talked Wilson over. But we must not blame Wilson too much. The negotiations were extended over a long period, and the people of U.S.A. were no longer interested in Europe. It displeased them to think that their President spent his time in the Hall of Mirrors instead of the White House. Wilson had little time to carry his points, and his power at home was on the wane. But this is no reason why we should not now try to make good the mistakes of those days.

Wilson saw what Clemenceau was aiming at, of course, for he remarked in April, 1919, that France's one interest in Poland was to weaken Germany. Lloyd George had intended to create a State composed of such Polish elements as wished to become part of such a State, and he made a statement to this effect on January 5th, 1918. It was not until after the Armistice that all these good principles were abandoned. Since it is never too late to mend, we might assure a lasting peace in East Europe by doing now what Lloyd George and Wilson had intended.

Following their various and undisputed acts of aggression against Germany (when they took Upper Silesia), Russia (when they nearly lost their own independence), and Lithuania (when they seized Vilna), the Poles settled down under Pilsudski, who came to power in May, 1926. Himself a great soldier, Pilsudski determined to assure peace. Polish aggression ceased. In fact, in the following year the Poles placed a resolution before the Eighth Assembly of the League of Nations at Geneva, demanding that "all attempts to make war as a means of settlement of international conflicts" were to be forbidden. In 1931 Poland proposed moral disarmament to the League.

And New Poland lived up to her word. There was, it is true, internal dissension. The minorities were not treated as one might have wished. But under Pilsudski there were great improvements. In 1932 Poland signed a Pact of Non-Aggression with Russia, and in 1934 with Germany.

Pilsudski stood for strict independence for Poland, not only nationally but also internationally. For this reason Poland rejected the Eastern Pact which would, in certain circumstances, have permitted foreign troops to pass through her territories.

Under Pilsudski, Poles living abroad began to return to their Fatherland, though the foreign minorities still tended to emigrate. No less than 53,783 emigrants were counted in 1935. The density of Poland's population is about 235 inhabitants per square mile at the moment of writing. This figure is likely to increase considerably since the population has risen by some five millions in the course of the last eleven years. Germany's increase of population in the same period was under four millions.

Mr. Chamberlain's pledge to assist Poland was given, to quote his precise words, "in the event of a clear threat to her independence which she considers it vital to resist with her national forces."

But is Danzig necessary to Poland's independence? Is the Corridor essential to the liberty of the Poles? Does Warsaw need to control the educational establishments of the Ukrainians in order to feel free? Must Upper Silesia be ruled by authorities foreign to the indigenous population to safeguard Polish rights?

Let us take one question at a time. Danzig is not at all necessary. Poland's trade, as I have shown through Polish statistics, does not depend upon Danzig and the Vistula at all. Danzig is a source of trouble to Poland and of unrest to the whole of Europe. It is admitted on all sides to be German, and can, under present circumstances, never become more than a thorn in the side of the Poles. Without Danzig, Poland would be richer and happier.

The Corridor is of importance to Poland, it is true, as an outlet to the sea. But that is all. The district is German, not Polish. Its loss would not affect Poland so long as she were assured a free port and harbour through which her goods might pass free from all duty. Without such a port, of course, the loss would be great. But with it there would really be no loss at all, save in nominal area.

Upper Silesia, like all industrial centres, is thickly populated and provides no outlet for Poland's surplus. Other and all-Polish industrial centres would actually benefit by an increase of trade, Poland's unemployment figures would drop, and increased prosperity would result. This also applies to Oderberg.

The Olsa area, which is Slovak, would not affect Poland at all. It is merely part of the land taken from Czecho-Slovakia at the end of last year.

Autonomy for the Ukrainians would end one of the most frequent causes of Poland's helplessness throughout the centuries - internal dissent.

Mr. Bilainkin has agreed to the need of something being done. In an article headed "Let us confer - now!" in the *Sunday Press* (June 18th, 1939) he wrote:

> "Have Poland and Germany not a good deal in dispute?
> "Will a rich, growing Germany always be content with East Prussia cut off from the mainland by a Polish Province? Is it feasible to think that a German city, even though wholly dependent on Polish trade and goodwill for its existence, will continue to be satisfied for ever with non-German customs officials in its midst?"

Even though this writer believes Danzig to be *wholly* dependent on Poland, he did not consider the City would be satisfied with that state of affairs for ever. But, of course, as I have shown, Danzig is no longer dependent only on Poland, else her army of unemployed would stretch from frontier to frontier.

The fact is that the reasons quoted for the *status quo* no longer apply; they are as dead as the dodo.

12

The small nationalities

But there are, on the other hand, many good reasons for intervening in the interests of small nationalities. Take the Ukrainians in Poland. I have referred in general to numerous acts of oppression throughout the centuries, and propose now to quote some specific examples.

Although the Ukrainians could vote, with a few exceptions, for the Sejm, they were prevented from sending too many of their own representatives to Parliament by the most ruthless measures. In summer 1930, when preparations were being made for the November elections, the anti-Ukrainian action began. For the Ukrainian faction was still the most powerful Parliamentary minority movement.

An excuse was easy to find, for there has been no peace in Polish Ukraine within living memory. At the end of August, 1930, fifty Polish farms went up in flames, and Ukrainians were blamed. The prisons in the cities were not large enough to hold the Ukrainian parliamentarians, priests, teachers, students and writers who were arrested. Crowds of prisoners arrived at the gaol gates every day. Cells soon housed from 12 to 20 Ukrainians, although at other times never more than five, as an absolute maximum, were confined in them. Trial before the Courts was omitted in thousands of cases. Here and there, the prisoners were simply shot out of hand, officially because they tried to escape. Remarkably enough, they were invariably killed and never wounded. The Ukrainian politician Holowinski was shot in this way. But all this did not prevent the Ukrainians from voting. Polish troops advanced against the villages.

A troop of men from the 14th Polish Ulan Regiment left Lemberg early in September, their objective being the village of Gaje. Like most villages in this part of the country (Galicia), Gaje was surrounded by trees. Nearing the village, they encountered peasants with their carts, driving along the middle of the road. The peasants, surprised, made way for the cavalcade. But the peasants did not doff their caps on seeing the military force, and one of the non-commissioned officers hit the foremost peasant in the face with a leather whip, leaving long, blood-red weals. The peasant fell from his seat into a ditch. Several other peasants speedily jumped down and two or three turned to the man in the ditch. Before they could reach him., Polish soldiers attacked them with whips. Ten minutes later, the troops continued their ride.

The mounted men stopped in front of the house of the local mayor. Mayor and councillors had to appear and to hand over a list of the inhabitants of the village. The village was sentenced to a community fine of 50 cwt. of oats, 1,000 eggs, 20 pigs, 50 cwt. of flour and 50 cwt. of a groat-like substance in common use in the Ukraine. Furthermore, the troops were to be given a full load of food, cigarettes, spirit and tobacco. The time limit was fixed at two hours.

Now Ukrainian villages are not rich as a rule. But they were told that if they did not bring the supplies within the two hours the soldiers would forage for themselves, and those with pretty wives and daughters trembled at the idea of Polish soldiery in their homes.

The supplies were collected, although it meant that the village would suffer bitter hardships afterwards. Then the peasants were made to assemble. Their clothing was torn off, and each of them was held by four soldiers, while others beat them without mercy. When they lost consciousness, pails of water were thrown over them. After a time, they were flung into one corner of the communal room, and the next batch was similarly treated. Incidentally, the lieutenant in command left this work to his subordinates.

This is a typical example though the process sometimes varied. In the village of Hrystyce, Lieut. Neumann called the councillors of the village. For four hours they had to stand at attention, and were beaten for the slightest movement. The mayor was asked who had arms, and on his replying that no one had any, he was given 50 blows on the naked body. The members of the council, whose names were Michael Lassaral, Alexander Lassaral, Wyszczanski, Turczyn, Wojtowicz, Olejnik, Burbel and Weres, were similarly treated. The authorities afterwards refused to receive the deputation from this village, when protest was to have been made.

In the village of Jaryczow, twenty peasants were whipped. In the village of Horodyslawice the whole Ukrainian library was destroyed, including religious works. Numerous villagers were also beaten up. In the village of Kurowce a peasant named Politacz, an old man, was beaten until he lost consciousness, then revived with pails of cold water, and forced to walk through the village barefooted. A Polish soldier rode on either side of him, a whip in his hand. In Mystowice, two women were also beaten until they were unconscious, but this outrage was perpetrated by the police, and not by soldiers. These police had bound bands round their caps, so that their numbers could not be recognised. It can be understood that the state of these and scores of other villages was ghastly after the troops retired. I have quoted the month in which all this was carried out on a wholesale manner, but cases enough have occurred at other times.

This anti-Ukrainian action was successful. The Ukrainian faction in the Sejm was much smaller at the following election. In some areas, only the Government candidates were proposed, none daring to nominate others.

It is hard to produce documentary proof of this brutality since in Poland there is no freedom of movement. Every foreigner has to register with the police through his hotel, and he has difficulties in seeing things for himself. I did see much, but did not take my camera further than Cracow as I had no wish to come into conflict with the authorities. To take a camera further into the South-East direction is tantamount to asking for arrest. Nobody troubled me in Cracow, but then the scenes of the outrages were all far away. In Lemberg things are stricter, and any foreigner seen in Ukrainian villages is an immediate object of suspicion. I visited some villages and was unquestionably lucky to escape trouble.

William Day, of the *Canadian Times,* visited the villages after the great work of destruction, and he photographed a village where the troops had spent several days. He also took pictures of peasants who had been tortured or injured. Nothing happened to him there, and he returned to Lemberg to dispatch his report and pictures. He was immediately arrested, his camera, plates and pictures seized, and he himself remained in a cell until the Consul secured his release. He was then compelled to leave the country at once. The charge against him was "Spreading information dangerous to the State."

The conditions in the prisons must be dreadful if the stories of the relations of Ukrainian prisoners are to be believed. But I did not see these prisons, so I can give no first-hand information. It is quite impossible to obtain permission to visit them. After these excesses, the Opposition in the Sejm asked pertinent questions, and also demanded an investigation into conditions in Lucz prison. The Polish Minister of the Interior replied that he had made enquiries, but that everything seemed to him to be in order at Lucz. A short time afterwards he actually informed Parliament that a prison officer had been punished there for stealing a gold watch from a prisoner. It is scarcely necessary to add that since 1930 the Ukrainians hate Warsaw.

It is hard to believe all this, as I readily admit. If I had not spoken with so many of the persons concerned, I should not believe it myself. The Polish officials I had to deal with were the most polite men I have ever met. At Posen, one accompanied me for half an hour to assist me with a ticket which required stamping when I broke my journey, bowing me into each office as we tried to find the right one. When I entered Poland, officials never asked me to show them my money, they immediately believed me when I said I had fifty pounds in banknotes and a cheque, and gave me a written confirmation, so that I could take part of it out again. When I went for a visa for Poland, I was given one free of charge, although it costs 25 zloty, and was bowed out, despite the fact that scores of others were waiting. I was treated with the greatest courtesy by the Polish officials everywhere. They did everything possible to make me feel at home. I have nothing but praise and gratitude for them personally. But I must record facts and not my feelings. I find it hard to explain that such kindly people are so brutal to their minorities. Such, however, is the simple fact.

White Russians, too, have told me dreadful things. In 1921 there were 514 White Russian schools in Poland. In 1925 there were 20. The remaining 494 were closed. In 1926 there were just three of these schools left.

A kind of guerrilla warfare has been waged for two decades between White Russians and Poles. Isolated Polish settlers dare not go out unarmed - even to-day, twenty years after the inclusion of the area in the Polish Republic. At first the White Russians were inclined to turn Bolshevik, in order to obtain Russia's help against the Poles; later they tried for independence.

On January 15th, 1927, the Polish police rounded up the White Russian leaders. Four members of the Sejm, who legally enjoyed immunity, among them Taraskiewicz, leader of the Hromada, with over a hundred prominent members of that Organisation, were arrested. On the same date 80 prominent White Russians were imprisoned in Warsaw. The headmasters and teachers of the White Russian schools were arrested or dismissed and the establishments closed. It was officially announced that the arrested men had been acting on behalf of the Komintern and had been engaged in revolutionary activities.

The White Russian peasants replied with desultory demonstrations. But they had no leaders, and were soon crushed. In a single day there were 11 casualties at Kossow, to quote but one example, including 5 dead. The organisations of the White Russians were then dissolved. Fifty-six White Russian leaders were brought up for trial at Vilna at the end of February, 1928, more than a year after their arrest. They included the four members of the Polish Parliament, the Sejm. Roughly six hundred witnesses appeared against them. After the case had lasted several months, 37 of the accused were sentenced to imprisonment for periods varying from three to twelve years. But the illegal Organisation of the White Russians is still alive. The men meet in secret. I was told some details, but only after I promised not to publish them, for the slightest hint as to the place concerned would, my informants said, lead to wholesale arrests and the ruin of thousands.

The following quotations show that this did not escape the Press. The *Daily Herald,* one of the journals whose writers use to attack Poland regularly, remarks, for example, that "not even Ireland in her worst days could show conditions so terrible as those in which the Polish peasants exist to-day" (*Daily Herald,* 23. 11. 1937). The "Polish peasants" were probably minorities.

The *Manchester Guardian* has also sponsored the case of the minorities under Polish rule: "In the autumn of 1930 the Polish Ukraine was 'pacified' by detachments of Polish cavalry and mounted police, who went from village to village arresting peasants and carrying out savage floggings and destroying property. The number of peasants who were flogged ran into many thousands" (*Manchester Guardian,* 10. 10. 1938).

The *Daily Express* observed that the Ukrainians were "held against their will. The union with the Poles was forced upon them. The Poles marched troops into the Ukrainian lands and staked their claims with bayonets. Since 1923 the 'Polonisation' of the Ukrainians has gone forward with a ferocity that recalls the 'pacification' of the old Turkish territories by the Bashi-Bazouks" (*Daily Express,* 12. 11. 1934).

Further West, the methods adopted against the minorities were marked by less physical brutality, but were nevertheless harsh. For example, the children of German-speaking parents in Upper Silesia who wished to attend German schools had to register between May 25th and 31st, 1926. Each child had to bring a statement in writing, signed by the parent or guardian, stating: "I declare that the child registered above belongs to the German language minority." That was not in accordance with the Geneva Convention. Only when no school existed in the area was a written application to be made, but this was simply overruled. Despite this, the number of applications was very large. I rather think the Poles were honestly surprised. Some people say they only pretended to be, but I doubt it. I am prepared to accept their astonishment as real.

But the methods adopted to reduce this total were unjust. Each parent or guardian was made to appear in person before the Polish authorities, who greeted them in Polish. Precisely 5,784 parents and guardians in the Kattowitz area were questioned, and the simple statements of the parents were not always accepted. It was then asserted that 145 of the children could not prove that they were Polish subjects, while 47 had applied to a school which was nearest their residence, but not in their proper district. There were also others who were struck from the list. In 391 cases the signatures were stated not to be correct. This was in the vast majority of cases because the mother had signed, whereas the Poles only accepted the mother's signature when the father was dead, or was otherwise incapable of signing. The subsequent statement of the fathers concerned that they were in agreement with the applications, and would append their signatures was not accepted. The applications were rejected. 1,307 pupils were struck from the list because the parents had failed to appear in person at the right time. 5,205 applications were rejected en masse, the claim being that they did not, in the opinion of the Polish authorities, belong to the minority.

The total number of applications made by fathers, mothers or guardians covered 8,560 children. Nor less than 7,114 were not permitted to attend the German schools. Articles 75 and 131 of the Geneva Convention were thus not adhered to. By 1928 the number of applications in the area under discussion had fallen to about 2,500 as a result of the difficulties. [The German minority in the] Kattowitz area was compelled to learn Polish at school, and to give up the right to study at German schools. Yet the people of Kattowitz still speak German, as

I have heard for myself. Even now, peace has not been restored. In the middle of July, 1939, I saw more police there than I had observed in the whole of Warsaw and, for the first time, I noticed mounted police. At one street corner, I even saw two mounted police who remained at their posts until relieved by two others. All day they remained there - perhaps all night as well, but I did not go to look.

At the 1928 elections, the Germans and other minorities returned numerous representatives to the Sejm, but afterwards the lists of electors were revised. In the electorate of Teschen-Bielitz, the whole list was declared to be out of order, and 20,000 votes cancelled by a stroke of the pen before the November elections of 1930. Some of the electors succeeded in registering their names for the new lists, but for the most part they were too late. The Polish authorities demanded that they should present a document affirming their Polish nationality. The police station was besieged, but in the few days left before the lists were closed only a few of the electors could obtain these certificates, the remainder losing their votes as a result.

Those at work found it difficult to apply in the hours fixed. A certain regulation was then interpreted by the local authorities to mean that a vote could be made in secret or openly, as desired, and a notice was printed in the Kattowitz journal *Polska Zachodnia* that those who voted secretly would be regarded as enemies of the State. Terrorism followed, and persons known to be of German descent were beaten up. In 1930 the Germans lost about 100,000 votes in Upper Silesia alone. No one who voted for the German list could hope to escape attack since the compartments in the election booths were torn down, and the votes had to be made before the eyes of the supervising Poles.

On November 9th of the same year groups of Poles from other areas, accompanied by local guides, smashed the doors of German residents, entered their rooms, and broke up the furniture. Sleeping people were dragged from their beds; those who had been wakened by the noise and who tried to save their property were beaten with sticks and rods. Some of the Germans escaped and appealed to the police who, however, claimed that they could do nothing as their numbers were too small. Two days later a similar attack was made on the Germans in the village of Golassowitz. A free fight followed, but the Poles outnumbered the local inhabitants. This was reported in the Polish Press as a revolt of the German-speaking inhabitants.

The German Minister of Foreign Affairs, Dr. Curtius, sent a request to the League of Nations, asking for help for the minority. That was on November 27th. A second note followed on December 9th.

But it was not until January 21st, 1931, that the League found time to discuss matters. The League used diplomatic but hard words, and demanded that the position of the Germans be improved. This should be clear enough proof that the charges against the Poles were not unfounded. It was established that the Polish Government had not even denied that such incidents had taken place. 255 cases were placed before the League.

Small wonder that I found the people of Upper Silesia only speaking German in low tones or in private. Small wonder that they look askance at strangers.

One must ask whether it is in keeping with the rights of small nations or nationalities that they should thus be included in States where they are exposed to such treatment. Poland has tried to make the minorities relinquish their language and customs; she has failed despite more than twenty years of activities such as I have described in this chapter. But the attempts are still going on. One begins to wonder whether the Ukrainians, White Russians and Germans should not also enjoy some protection from England, or must it only be the Poles?

13

Treatment of minorities

Though disputes between the Poles and their minorities were considered probable when the Polish frontiers were fixed, they were not expected to be of such far-reaching consequences as actually proved to be the case. According to the *Handbook of Central and East Europe*, published by the Central European Times Publishing Co. at Zurich, Danzig is "under international control and a High Commissioner appointed by the League of Nations is supposed to decide disputed questions between Poland and Danzig." The fact that a High Commissioner was "supposed" to decide disputed questions clearly shows that disputes were regarded as extremely likely, else why the provision?

The answer is that at the beginning of 1919 the Danzigers demanded union with the Reich, so that the Free City arrangement was known all along to be against their wishes, and the customs union with Poland was equally known to oppose their desires. This handbook claimed (in 1935) that the 22.2 million Poles formed 69.1% of the whole population of Poland. Even this figure would show minorities totalling over 30%, but it is, of course, based on the official Polish statistics, and I have already shown the methods used by Poland in the Ukraine and Upper Silesia to secure a high percentage of registered Poles and a low percentage of foreign minorities. That I only selected two areas is not because there are no further cases, but because a description of those methods in other parts does not need illustration, being the same in type.

The same handbook throws an interesting light on the school system. There are (page 579 of the handbook) 1,765 nursery schools where the language used is Polish, 47 with Ukrainian, 34 with German, 42 with Yiddish, 35 with Hebrew, 2 with French, 2 with Russian and 16 which are bi-lingual, Polish being one of the languages. These figures apply to 1929-1930, and the number of non-Polish schools has dropped further since then. But even accepting these figures it is obvious that the proportion is wrong.

It means that 1,765 such schools exist of which only well below 10% teach in languages other than Polish, while according to the same handbook over 30% of the population is non-Polish.

Other similar conditions are noted in the other schools. There are actually, the handbook states, 22 academic schools, of which all, without exception, are Polish. But, worst of all, the teachers' training colleges are practically all Polish. Of 229 such establishments only 10 taught in Ukrainian and 3 in German. On page 580 the handbook asserts that of 100,500 pupils at nursery schools, as many as 93,700 are given instruction only in Polish.

When we come to organisations of a voluntary character, founded without the help of the State, the proportion is very different. The handbook (p. 556) shows that at the end of 1933 there were 6,421 Polish co-operative societies, while those of the national minorities amounted to no less than 5,341, of which 3,411 were Ukrainian. In other words, the Ukrainians had more than half as many as the Poles, but only because co-operative societies could be founded without State aid, while schools could not.

The need of more Ukrainian and German schools is beyond dispute, yet the authorities are doing their best to reduce the already meagre total. All this is in direct opposition to the terms under which Poland was given the minority areas. The Poles persuaded the Allies that they would care for all their minorities, and their word was accepted. It has turned out that this was a mistake. If the Poles really gave the minorities equal opportunities we should find a proportion of Ukrainian and

German schools at least equal to the proportion of Ukrainians and Germans admitted by official Polish statistics. In point of fact it requires a brave man to send his son or daughter to a non-Polish school - and he is, moreover, probably exposing his child to difficulties in after-life. The Poles have finely calculated this factor, and it has been fairly successful in achieving its purpose.

But we must not believe that the number of children speaking Polish is conclusive evidence. There are hundreds of thousands who speak two languages - Polish, which they are compelled to learn at school, and their own, taught by their mothers at home and spoken in secrecy. This may appear fantastic to those who are not acquainted with Eastern Europe, but how else can one explain, for example, the fact that the Ukrainian language has survived all attempts for centuries to stamp it out?

It is astonishing that so much Ukrainian, German, Polish, Lithuanian and, as a matter of fact, one or two other languages, such as Slovakian, are still spoken at all. The Ukrainians remained in their native areas, so far as they were not imprisoned or sent to Warsaw under protest. But the Germans who decided to retain their Reich nationality knew, when they did so, that they would have to leave hearth and home. They automatically became foreigners in their own country. Nothing can be said against this. The persons concerned voted for German nationality fully knowing what would result. It was hard on them to have to choose between their homes and their true country, of course.

But the worst part came afterwards, when the Poles informed numerous German-speaking land-owners that they were not Polish citizens, and could not, therefore, continue to be farmers in the Republic. Small-holders were less affected, but big German land-owners suffered severely. In many cases the fact that a son had studied at a university in Prussia was regarded as rendering the whole family ineligible for Polish nationality, and it must be remembered that the areas where the farmers lived had been a part of Prussia until 1919.

The Germans belonged in many cases to a league for maintaining language and tradition, known as the *Deutschtumsbund,* in the first years of the Republic. At the beginning of August, 1923, the police raided all the branches of this *Bund*. Within three days not a single branch was left. The Polish Press reported that the organisation had been aiming at high treason. But none of the leaders of the *Deutschtumsbund* was brought up for trial. Hundredweights of printed matter were collected at the Posen Court, but the case was "pending" for years, and nothing came of it.

Nevertheless, the Polish action achieved its purpose, for the *Deutschtumsbund* had been handling the complaints of the German minority, and the material collected, intended in part for Geneva, was destroyed when the organisation was broken up.

The Germans whose property was seized received compensation, it is true. But the amounts were ridiculously small. Baron Firck's property at Radolin, known to be worth several million gold zloty, was officially valued at only 250,000 gold zloty; the big Hindersin estates, at Lissa, had been officially estimated at 451,000 dollars, but the official valuation when it came to expropriation was 40,000 dollars. I quote these two examples because the estates were fairly well known, but less famous property fared no better.

The extent of the expropriation may be seen from the statement of the (Polish) Liquidation Commission on May 27th, 1929, i.e. that 4,000 country estates and 2,000 plots of land in municipal areas had been "liquidated."

Those who had not received the documents confirming the cession of real estate in German provinces during the War were particularly unlucky. The applications had been filed at the Courts in the manner usual in Prussia at the time, but shortage of staff owing to the continuation of hostilities had led to postponement of registration. German ownership of real property is entered in a book called the *"Grundbuch."* In normal times this procedure is fairly speedy, but in the War years it was often held over till peace time.

In the areas taken over by the Poles, failure to produce a document was regarded as a reason for driving the owners from the land. The fact that the applications had in many cases been pending for years was not taken into consideration. The Poles said they were the successors of the Prussians, and must drive away all who had no document to confirm ownership. Precisely 3,964 German settlers were robbed of their land in this way, and became homeless. They received no compensation.

These 3,964 settlers were summarily turned out. But in thousands of other cases action was also taken against German peasants and landowners on account of their racial origin. One method was as follows:

The Prussian Government had financially assisted many of the smallholders to buy land, and possessed, until such time as the payments were completely returned, the right to buy the holders out. Before the Treaty of Versailles came into effect, Prussia had transferred its claims to the German Peasants' Bank at Danzig. But Poland claimed to have taken over the right along with sovereignty of the provinces in question. I shall not go into the rights and wrongs of the claims of the Danzig Bank and the Polish State, which are really immaterial. The point is that the Poles used this opportunity to dispossess the Germans forcibly. When a smallholder died, his lawful heirs were not allowed to take over his property, which was claimed by the Polish Government as its own. This meant no compensation at all. The owner could sell during his lifetime, but only Poles were allowed to buy from him, and the price was kept down to an absurd level. Hundreds of these cases were brought before the Courts, often before International Courts, but no redress was made until 1929, and even then it only affected those who had not been robbed of their land in the meanwhile.

14

Upper Silesia's example

It may not be without interest to consider how Poland came into possession of much of the territory now under her control. Upper Silesia is an excellent example, all the more so since its inclusion in the Polish Republic was against the wishes of the British Government in general, and of Lloyd George in particular.

A plebiscite was to be held in Upper Silesia, and Woiczech Korfanty was nominated Poland's Commissar for the Plebiscite. One of his closest collaborators was a lawyer called Wolny, which is the Polish word for "free," or "at liberty." The plebiscite was held on March 21st, 1921. Germany received 707,393 votes and Poland 479,365 votes, despite the fact that it was well known that high taxes would be necessary in Germany in order to pay the Reparations, and despite considerable pressure on the part of the Poles. This was a fairly good majority, and the Inter-Allied Commission at Oppeln was of the opinion that the question was settled, for this plebiscite was to have been considered final. The French General le Rond, who was in close touch with Korfanty, favoured a return to Poland. The promises made to the population of Upper Silesia by Korfanty place all election pledges in the shade. There was little he did not promise them if they would vote for Poland. And yet the Germans obtained a good majority.

Korfanty should never have been allowed to act as Plebiscite Commissar, for he had tried to take control illegally on two occasions, the last being on August 19th, 1920, when General le Rond ordered the French to disarm the German police, and Korfanty was equipped with a good supply of arms and munitions from some quarter or other.

On May 2nd, 1921, Korfanty, while still officially holding the post of Plebiscite Commissar, began a night march against the area. The districts of Beuthen, Pless, Rybnik, Gross-Strelitz, Gleiwitz and Kattowitz were taken by storm. The German police had been in part replaced by Polish police. The latter joined the rebels in uniform, and the former were disarmed, in numerous cases ill-treated, and in many actually murdered.

Between 50 and 60 persons were murdered during that night. German officials were arrested and mishandled. Where French soldiers were on duty, they took no action whatever. The protests of the Germans reached General le Rond, who ignored them. The Polish Government relieved Korfanty, it is true, of his post as Commissar, but it was too late. Korfanty then sent a message to Lloyd George, Briand, Harding, Lord Curzon, Count Sforza and Giolitti, telling them that he had done his best to prevent a rising. Korfanty was in possession, however.

The Italian troops endeavoured to restore law and order (there were no Fascists in those days, and no Axis), and they marched on May 4th from Ratibor towards Rybnik. The Poles fired on these representatives of the Allied troops, and the Italians suffered 30 killed and some 50 wounded.

Fighting followed. The inhabitants resisted the Polish insurgents. The Poles cut off the water and electricity supply of Kattowitz for several days in succession, and the infant mortality rose alarmingly. Families filled all imaginable vessels with water after that, and were thus better able to withstand attempts to torture them by cutting off their water supply, which were repeated several times.

England never agreed to all this. The French troops stood and looked on, but England never countenanced the Polish brutality. That is a fact of which we may be justly proud. The British member of the Inter-Allied Commission at Oppeln, Colonel Percival, sent dispatches containing the truth to London. They completely contradicted the tales told by the Poles and the French. On May 13th, 1921, Lloyd George told the House of Commons that the Inter-Allied Commission had intended to give Poland the parts of Upper Silesia which had voted with a majority for that country, and he characterised the armed action of the Poles as a complete breach of the Treaty of Versailles. Lloyd George emphasised that this breach of faith on the part of the Poles would lead the Germans to grumble that they had to abide by the Treaty, while other nations did not. He stressed the fact that while some might say they were "only Germans," they, too, had a right to whatever the Treaty granted them. Lloyd George also said it would be unfair not to allow the Germans to make use of their own troops to restore order, and his words were loudly applauded in the House. England, he went on, stood for fair play. He also remarked that the area in question had been German for two centuries, and that it had certainly not been Polish for the past six hundred years.

But fighting continued. England did not fight for the weaker party, nor, of course, could she be expected to, for, after all, we had troubles enough of our own. But it would be a crime if we were to march to-day to defend Polish possession of the area taken by Korfanty against the Inter-Allied Commission, against the Treaty of Versailles, and against the plebiscite. General le Rond finally threatened to send 15,000 men, with tanks and heavy artillery, to aid the insurgents against the inhabitants. This forced the Germans to abandon their resistance.

Poland had to return some of the area, including Beuthen and Gleiwitz, but retained Kattowitz, Pless, Rybnik, Lublinetz, Tarnowitz, and Königshütte. About a million Upper Silesians came under the rule of Warsaw as a result. The area ceded to Poland, despite the plebiscite, included nine of the 14 rolling mills, 53 of the 65 coal pits, 23 of 37 furnaces, 15 of 25 steel works, and rich mineral deposits (coal, zinc and lead).

Thirty-one railway lines and 45 highways were cut through by the new frontier in order to give the Poles what property they wanted, such as the new model hospital at Rudahammer. It was a victory of brute force.

It is frequently forgotten that the plebiscite I have mentioned was not to decide whether Upper Silesia should be divided or not. It was to vote the whole compact area either to Poland or Germany. This view was held everywhere. 59.64 per cent. of the votes were given in favour of continuing the union with Germany, and only 40.36 per cent. for Poland. With one exception, every town had a clear German majority. Rural districts voted, strangely enough, with a German majority where British or Italian troops were stationed, and only when French soldiers, under General le Rond's eye, were in occupation did the people in the country favour union with Poland.

The majority had spoken and, in accordance with our Democratic system, a clear majority should have sufficed to secure Upper Silesia for the Reich. Despite this, the Paris Conference awarded 1,235 square miles of territory (30% of Upper Silesia) with a population of 892,547 (42.6% of that of all Upper Silesia) to Poland. The most surprising part of the whole affair was that the Poles did not obtain a majority even with the help of Korfanty. But it became clear soon afterwards that the 40% Polish votes had been largely recorded for fear of Polish vengeance. The best example was at the elections in the part of Upper Silesia remaining German. 195,317 persons there had voted for union with Poland, but on December 7th, 1924, only 42,051 of them recorded votes for the Polish People's Party, the remainder voting for German parties.

This cannot be explained away by claims of Nazi oppression. At that time there were no National Socialists in this district at all. The authorities were Liberal, Democratic, of the Catholic Centre Party in the Reich, and the local boards were elected in the same manner as in London.

The partitioning of Upper Silesia left towns cut off from their natural source of supply.

I know this area well, but a brief description of just one sector of the new frontier may be of interest. Beuthen, a purely German town, ends in the middle of a railway station. In a tunnel under the platforms, Polish and German officials stand all day examining the papers of those who have to go from one side of the railway line to the other. One can book a ticket from German Beuthen to Polish-owned Kattowitz, for example, but one must possess a passport or a permit to reach the platform. One must walk past the German officials, who examine the papers, then past the Polish officials. Thousands of people live on one side and work on the other. Some live on one side, their fathers and mothers on the other. A passport or frontier permit is required to visit them. Purely German communities were divided by this frontier.

But the main point to consider is that Poland seized Upper Silesia with the aid of Korfanty, the chief official Polish Commissar at the plebiscite, afterwards officially disowned, and with the tacit consent of the French troops under le Rond. It was an act of aggression against the German population, and a flagrant breach of the Treaty of Versailles. Lloyd George confirmed it, the whole House of Commons applauded his words.

If it was wrong to seize this land we should hardly be right sending our troops to help the Poles perpetuate the wrong. It would be an absurd situation.

It must not be forgotten that the Province of Silesia belonged to Austria for many centuries. It passed into the possession of Prussia for the first time in 1763, but this merely meant exchanging one German Government, with its seat in Vienna, for another, with H.Q. in Berlin. From 1763 to 1921 Silesia remained part of Prussia. After Bismarck founded the Reich, of course, it was, with the rest of Prussia, included in what was then called the German Empire. But it was part of Austria first, then of Prussia and, finally, with the latter, of the Reich. This had no connection with Poland.

Upper Silesia is not part of the territory which belonged to Poland and which passed into the possession of another land following the triple partition of Poland. Indeed, it was already Prussian before the first partition of 1772. It could not, therefore, be regarded as rightfully belonging to the Poles at all.

Let us, by all means, guarantee the rightful claims of the Poles to Polish country. Let us assure Warsaw that we shall defend the ethnographical frontiers of Poland, if needed. But let us not spill British blood to defend artificially created borders, which owe their existence to twentieth-century brigandage. The story of Polish aggression in Upper Silesia, in the Ukraine and elsewhere is without a parallel in modern times.

In guaranteeing the present artificial frontiers of the Composite State of Poland we should be giving the Poles carte-blanche to continue to oppress their large minorities. In fact, we might even find ourselves in the unenviable position of having to dispatch our own soldiers to assist Warsaw in crushing the rebellious minorities within her borders!

In considering the sacred rights of small nationalities we must be as fair to the Ukrainians, the Lithuanians, the Germans and the White Russians as to the Poles. Our guarantees to Poland would then obviously be restricted to what rightfully belongs to Poland.

15

Conclusions

The Poles deserve their independence and they must not be allowed to share the fate of the Czechs. There can be no doubt on that point. But on the other hand it would be a mistake to let them think that we are prepared to support any and every claim they may choose to make.

It is a fine thing to be ready to fight for the independence of small nations, and deserves every praise. But that is a very different thing from fighting to enable a small nation to maintain the upper hand over foreign peoples.

We should, I fully believe, guarantee Poland's Polish frontiers, but we cannot be expected to fight in order that Warsaw may retain a customs union with Danzig, especially when the value of commerce passing through the Free State is constantly falling. If we do fight for Poland, no one will ever be able to say we did so for selfish reasons, for our interests lie overseas, not in East Europe. Indeed, we should be acting against our own interests by concentrating our forces in Eastern Europe. But that only serves to show we are unselfishly risking everything to assist others.

So far as Polish territory is concerned, this is laudable, if not quite in keeping with the axiom that "charity begins at home," and not quite what our overseas Dominions might reasonably expect of us. But when it is a matter of fighting in order that non-Polish territory may remain under Polish control, that is not so laudable. It would be against our own interests and against the principles of self-determination if we fought to make Danzig Polish.

I have travelled extensively in Poland, have talked with thousands of people there, and know almost every inch of the country. I know the purely Polish as well as the predominantly German and Ukrainian areas, and have questioned the people as to their wishes.

Danzig is German. The elections alone prove this. I have quoted the opinions of famous men. No one can deny that the vast majority of the Danzigers are Germans, or that they wish to join Germany. But if the Poles believe to the contrary, why not hold a plebiscite under English control and abide by the decision? Warsaw would, as I was told there, refuse such a solution, knowing the result in advance. Poles told me that this was not a fair test since they had claims to the mouth of the Vistula. But I have dealt with those claims in an earlier chapter, and can only repeat that such arguments would be equivalent to giving the Dutch estuary of the Rhine to Germany, or the Portuguese area around the Tagus to Franco Spain.

There is no sense in fighting to keep one group of Germans in Danzig from joining another group of Germans in the Reich. It would be tantamount to some other country going to war to prevent England and New Zealand from sharing a single government if they wanted to. Danzig, as a city, was founded by Germans. That Slavs may, many centuries ago, have opened a trading centre on the site of the present Free City is no reason for giving the area to Poland. The Serbs are also Slavs, and one might as well award it to them, for we have no proof that the Poles are the descendants of such Slavs. Indeed, historians declare they are not. But this point is not even of academic interest, and if we base claims on ancient days of occupation, we may as well begin by presenting the East coast of England to Denmark, for it belonged to the Danes long after the Slavs who may have founded a trading centre in the Danzig region had migrated. Imagine Germany - or for that matter France, Russia, or Italy - wishing to guarantee Denmark the East coast of England on historic grounds! The historical side of the argument could not be denied - but its utter absurdity would make all Europe laugh. Strangely enough, the equally absurd Danzig claim made by the Poles is taken quite seriously in many quarters.

The Corridor is also historically and geographically part of Germany. The main population, apart from the families settled there since 1918, is German by descent and language. Furthermore, this Corridor is as necessary for Germany as, say, the strip of territory from Bristol to Weymouth is to us. Imagine what our communications would be like if a broad strip of land from the Bristol Channel to the English Channel were in the possession of the Poles (or the Germans, or any other foreigners). Motorists would be unable to drive to Cornwall and Devon without permission of the English Corridor Power; they would only be able to travel by rail "by courtesy of the foreign Power concerned"; they would be unable to pass through on foot without a passport and a visa, and could not ask officials the way because the officials would all have no knowledge of English. Then if the foreign Power failed to repair the roads, so that communications were extremely bad, we should be forced to keep in touch with our "South-Western Provinces" by ship - which is precisely what Germany has to do to maintain communications with East Prussia. The parallel holds good in a geographical sense, but the Germans have to travel further by ship than we should require to. As this corner of England is still inhabited by the descendants of many Kelts, the racial claim to separate it from the rest of England would as a matter of fact be much stronger than a similar claim in the case of East Prussia, which is more German than Cornwall is Anglo-Saxon. The Corridor must be returned to Germany. It is only a source of trouble, as far-seeing British politicians predicted in 1919, when the subject was under discussion.

On the other hand, the Poles should be guaranteed a free harbour and port, so that their goods can pass through free from duty or customs control. That seems only fair. It is true that neither the Swiss nor the Hungarians have been treated so generously, but there are twice as many Poles as Hungarians, and a free outlet of this kind might reasonably be expected.

One may argue that this would place Poland's foreign trade at the mercy of Germany, but the truth is that this is already the case. The Germans could, at any moment, cut Poland off from the sea. Military forces could seal up the Corridor or, alternatively, the German navy could blockade the coast within a few hours. The small Polish navy would be quite helpless. There is thus no point in such an argument. Further, Poland, in normal times, exports comparatively little by way of the sea. I found the Vistula being principally used for swimming in warm weather, and saw more rowing-boats than commercial craft. One had the definite impression that the Vistula and Danzig can hardly be Poland's main trading outlets. Nor are they. Timber provides a good example. The amount of timber passing the Vistula in the form of rafts totalled 214,367 tons in 1912, but had fallen to 66,622 tons by 1938. Iron going upstream totalled 26,721 tons in 1913, while there was none at all on the Vistula in 1938; corresponding figures for petroleum were 41,887 tons in 1913 and none whatever in 1938, the last available figures.

Highly illuminating are the official Polish figures. In the year 1924, 10.9 per cent. of Poland's overseas exports were carried by waterways; in 1937 this figure had fallen to precisely 4 per cent., and in 1938 the total was only 2.3 per cent. In other words, the importance of waterways to Poland is dropping from year to year. The reason is that the Poles are not water-minded; they have promoted and fostered the railways and neglected water transport. I do not blame them for this. They never have been seamen and never will be. They have no objection to spending an hour in a rowing-boat, but they do not feel at home on the sea. Nor should we be if we had never had a coast of our own. But should we fight to retain for the Poles a coastline and the mouth of the Vistula, which the Poles themselves value less from year to year?

To give a comparison, 25 per cent. of the goods transported in Germany are conveyed by water; the corresponding figure for France is 20 per cent.; but in Poland, where the railway network is poorer than in either of the other lands mentioned, the amount of goods carried by water is less than 1 per cent.

The Corridor is German by population, as well as historically and geographically. It is only a source of trouble to the Poles. Let it be given back to the Germans.

Posen, the whole province as well as the town, has now in my opinion a Polish majority. I have gone into this question very carefully, and have toured the whole area. There is no doubt that it formerly was German. Its buildings nearly all bear an unmistakably German stamp. About half the people in some districts speak German, and, here and there, one finds more Germans than Poles. The German population left Posen after it became Polish, however, whenever possible. The Germans still left are a part of the pre-war population. Posen should have been left to Germany. But I see no sense in taking all Posen from Poland to-day. True, the original population was forced to leave, and Poles were settled there instead. But the majority in parts is now Polish, and the individuals are not responsible for what has happened. It was wrong to drive the Germans away, but to move the Poles who have settled there in the meanwhile would be unjust to them as individuals, while to place them all under German rule would only sow the seeds of future discord. Posen should be divided, the Western and purely German parts being returned, but the Eastern and mixed areas being left to Poland. The precise extent of the changes could be fixed on ethnographical lines, while an exchange of population afterwards would help to improve matters. Neither Poland nor Germany can expect to have everything their own way, and just as the Poles must abandon their claims to the German parts, so must the Germans agree to leave the Polish parts of former Posen to Poland, despite an excellent historical claim to the whole province. Peace must be assured by the simplest measures, and the arrangements must be of a character which will stand the test of time.

There is one other small area to which the Germans are entitled, and which England had intended them to have. That is Upper Silesia, illegally invaded, as I have shown, by the Poles long after peace had been officially proclaimed. This includes the German towns of Königshütte and Kattowitz, while Oderberg comes under the same category. I was in this area for some time, and toured the towns. The area is German-built. Some Poles have since settled there, and some Germans have crossed the frontier. But vast numbers still remain. I must repeat that the visitor may easily be led astray by the fact that the officials speak only Polish. The same applies to tourist offices, railway officials, and post office clerks. But the simple people are mainly German. Upper Silesia only became Polish because the Poles annexed it as a rich industrial area. That act of aggression on the part of the Poles was everywhere condemned at the time, especially by the British Labour Party, whose supporters repeatedly demonstrated against Poland in front of the Polish Embassy in London.

The Olsa area, small in extent, was awarded to Poland, as I have already mentioned, when Czecho-Slovakia fell. This district is Slovak, and should be returned to the Slovaks. The Poles gained possession of it only at the end of 1938, and they have done practically nothing there since, so that it would be no loss to them. This minor readjustment of a recently drawn frontier would assure friendly feeling between Poland and Slovakia. The Slovaks feel the loss of this strip of land, which again means that relations are separated from each other by an artificial frontier, very keenly.

The Ukrainian question, of course, cannot be settled by simply returning the Ukrainian area to any State, for these people have no country, although they are more numerous than the Spaniards or even the English in Europe. But this minority, the largest in Poland, and living in compact areas, must be given widest autonomy. It would probably prove necessary for an autonomous Ukraine to remain in the Polish customs area; in military matters, too, it would weaken Poland too much if the Ukraine were to be set up as a separate entity. The problem might be solved by incorporating all-Ukrainian regiments, under their own officers, in the Polish army. As regards their churches, schools, Press, sports organisations, hospitals, and social institutions generally, the Ukrainians should have complete independence. This would save Poland considerable trouble by ending the disorders in this part of the country, and stabilise her general position.

The strength of a chain is its weakest link, and Poland's weakness is that she has too many enemies within - enemies, because they are made to live as though they were Poles when they have no such wish. When one remembers that about three-sevenths of the population of Poland is non-Polish, one realises the magnitude of the danger. The Germans want to return to the Reich, the Ukrainians want their autonomy, the White Russians wish for more autonomy, the Jews are directly at variance with the State. It is the old story of a house divided against itself. For a time the Poles may be able to maintain the *status quo* by force of military display, but this cannot last long. Financial difficulties were noticeable on my visit in July, 1939, and everyone said that things could not go on in that manner.

Poland would lose very little territory by this arrangement, for Danzig is not part of Poland at all, and the Corridor is quite small, while Upper Silesia is a small strip of land on the frontier. Poland would lose practically no Polish citizens, whilst the benefits would be considerable. Tension would disappear, trade with Germany would be resumed, the army could be demobilised, and Poland could gradually build up her prosperity.

There would, however, have to be no mistake about what is Poland this time. England and France would have to guarantee the real Polish frontiers, and I do not see why we should not demand that Germany, Italy and the United States do the same. That is to say, we should have to make it a condition that the Corridor, Danzig and Upper Silesia could only be returned to Germany after Berlin had joined London and Paris in guaranteeing the new frontiers irrespective of what future internal changes might take place in Poland. And we could make it perfectly clear that we should in all circumstances defend the new frontier.

This would meet the needs of Poland. She would retain all her genuinely Polish territory, have her free port (which we should also guarantee if desired), and suffer no trading restrictions.

Clemenceau undoubtedly knew that the Corridor solution was not a good one, but he hoped that Germany would not become powerful until the Poles had settled their own people there, and thus assured a Polish majority. Germany regained her power before the Poles had succeeded in doing that, except in parts of Posen.

It must not be imagined that this solution meets all the German wishes. On the contrary, the Germans, not unnaturally, think they are entitled to all Posen - as in a sense they are. But a compromise is always the best solution, and I have no doubt whatever that both Berlin and Warsaw would accept the plan I have outlined if it were laid down as the basis of a round-table conference.

Purely German areas would go to the Reich; Posen, now settled with so many Poles, would be ethnographically divided, and the Ukrainians would enjoy a measure of autonomy which - though not nearly so great as that we grant our Dominions, or hardly that enjoyed by the Scots - would be an immeasurable improvement on the present state of affairs. Such a settlement would be absolutely in accordance with the self-determination principle, upon which the peace treaties were to have been based, and would assure peace in East Europe not only in our time but for many generations to come.

16

Facsimile Appendix

Scans of pages 160-167 of the original 1939 book.

" But each of you has in his soul the seeds of the future rights and the extent of the future frontiers."

—Adam Mickiewicz.

▰▰▰ The Western historic boundaries of Poland.
▬▬▬ The present boundaries of Poland.

This map, which takes the place of a picture postcard (the back was printed as such) is widely distributed for propaganda purposes in Poland. An inflated Poland, stretching to the very doors of Berlin, is depicted. The " historical boundaries " are intended to awaken the impression that Poland is entitled to these areas in the West. The eastern boundaries on the same " historical basis " have tactfully been omitted, so as to avoid offending the Eastern neighbours.

One unconsciously asks whether Poland believes that British blood should be shed to defend these imaginary frontiers—especially since the demarcation of such boundaries would unquestionably lead to more wars. The quotation shows that the " historic frontiers " are regarded rather more from the point of view of the future than of the past.

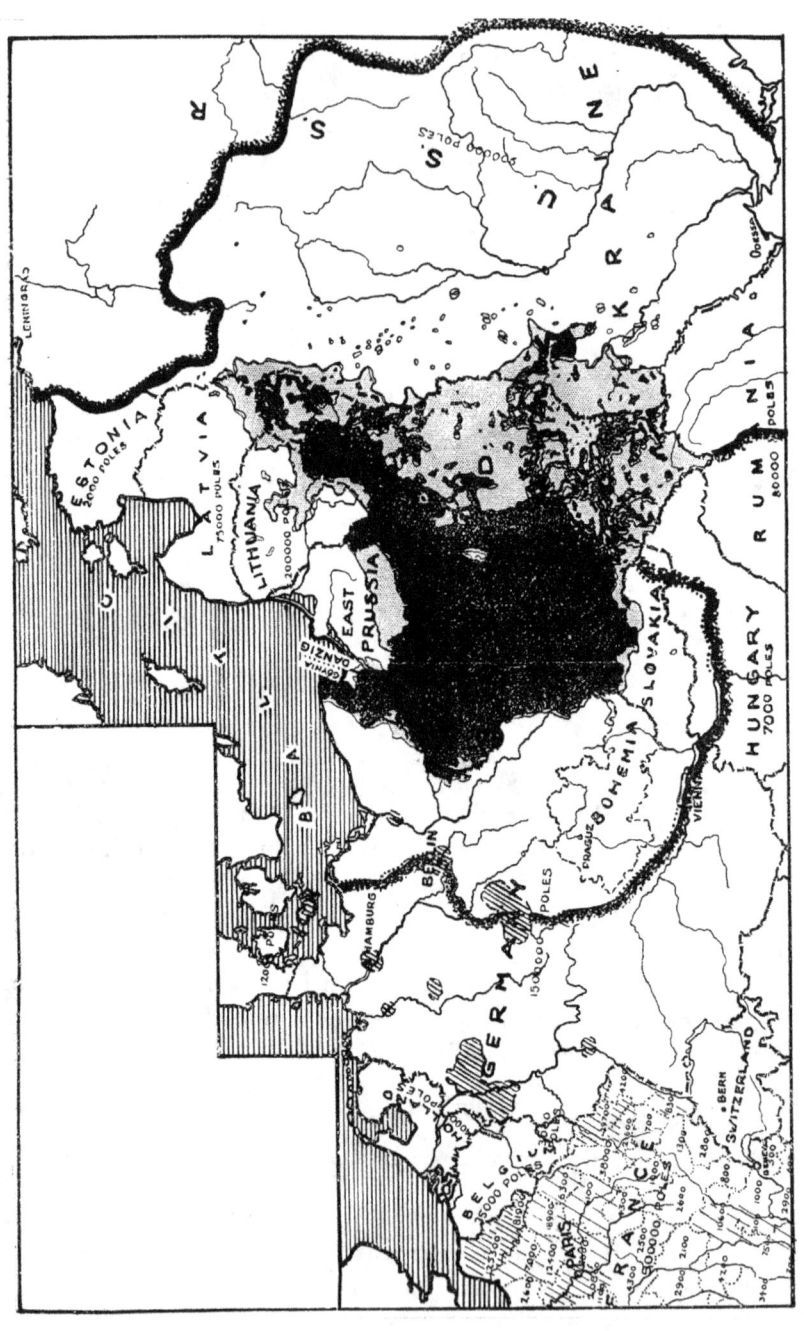

Map showing the distribution of the Poles in Poland and in the neighbouring countries of Europe.
Reference.

▮	Poles in the majority.
▯	Poles in the minority.
~~	Outline of the farthest extent of the Polish State in the course of the centuries.
▰	Comparatively large number of Poles in Germany and Denmark.
/////	Over 50,000 Poles in one French département.
/////	Over 20,000 ,, ,, ,, ,, ,,
////	Over 5,000 ,, ,, ,, ,, ,,
1000	Number of Poles in one département.
······	Département borders.
⌒⌒	State frontiers.

This map is based on official data and statistics. It shows the actual position clearly. Broad stretches of land, which belonged to the Rzeczpospolita for centuries, are to be seen on it. It will also be seen that present-day Poland, which is precisely in the heart of the historical lands, is situated where the Polish element is in a majority.

Present-day Poland is thus the kernel, the rest of the " Polish land " lies in neighbouring States—according to Warsaw. The former frontiers are drawn to include Lithuania, Latvia and Esthonia, East Prussia, Danzig, and such odd stretches of territory as Germany (as far as Berlin) and former Czecho-Slovakia, with the boundary just north of Budapest. A big slice of Russia completes the claim. But, as though to show that these claims were really somewhat modest, the Polish minority is recorded in the area of Dortmund, Essen, Cologne —and the North of France, as far as the English Channel! Hamburg, a Danish Island, and a few other " minority Polish areas " complete this designation. The percentage of Poles in these districts is in most cases lower than that of French or Italians in London, or coloured persons in Cardiff. Such maps have, absurd as it may seem, attracted no little attention in Poland, where the less educated citizens accept the claims as well founded.

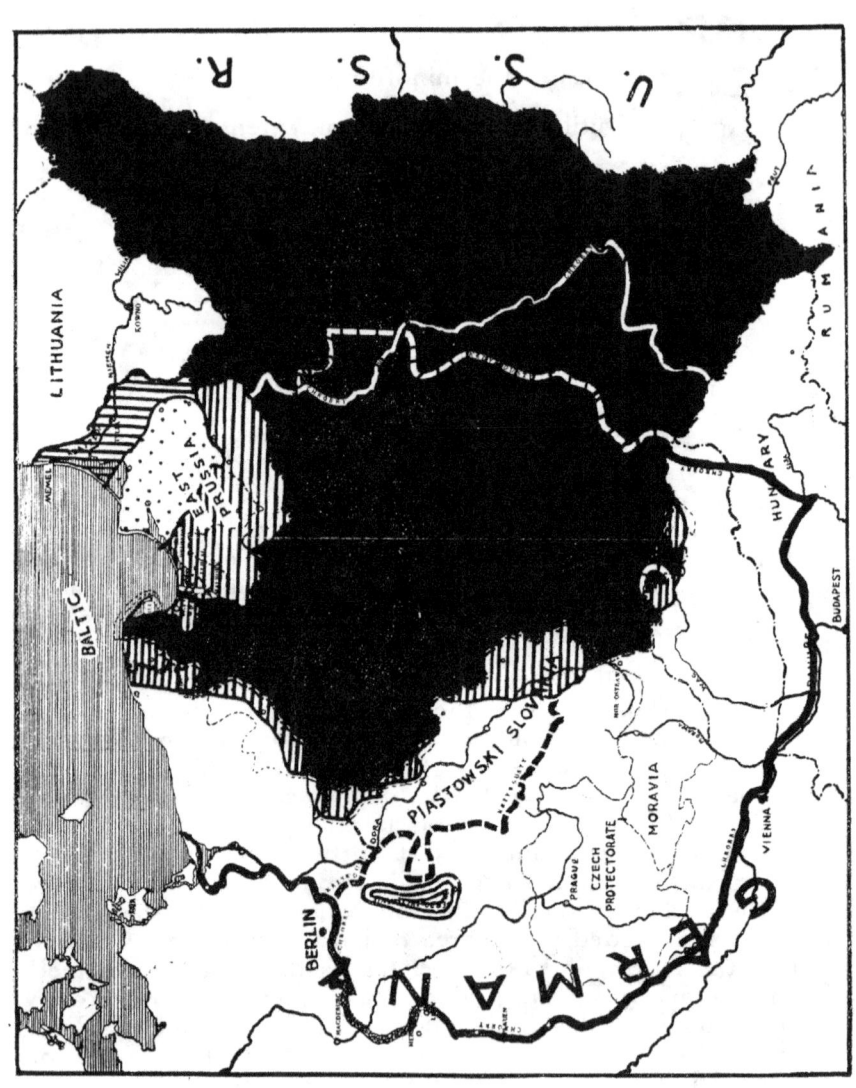

The Western frontiers of Poland in history, and the altered frontiers of the neighbouring States since September 1938.

According to Jan Marski.

- - - Present State frontiers.

- - - - Present frontiers of the Protectorate Bohemia-Moravia, and frontiers of the Free State of Danzig.

 Extent of the present Wendic (Sorbic-Lausatian) enclave.

Western frontier of Poland at the time of Boleslaw the Bold (A.D. 1025).

 Western frontier of Poland at the time of Boleslaw the Wrymouthed (A.D. 1138).

=1657= Western frontier of the Pommeranian districts of Lauenberg and Bütow, which belonged to Poland until 1657.

- - - - - Western frontier of Poland before the partition of 1772.

Frontiers demanded by Poland at the Peace Conference at Versailles (note of the Polish Delegation to M. Jules Cambon, 28.11.1919).

Areas and frontiers directly demanded for Poland, without any plebiscite or reserve.

Areas and frontiers demanded by Poland for Lithuania, and, in case of a union of Lithuania with Poland, directly for Poland.

 Remainder of the area of East Prussia, for which Poland demands independence under the protection of the League of Nations (on similar lines to the Free State of Danzig).

A large part of Europe would have to be carved up to meet the demands of the Poles, as illustrated in this map. Big slices of neighbouring countries, where the population is 99.9 per cent. German, for example, are demanded without a plebiscite. This is not so absurd as it might seem—for with a plebiscite, the Poles would hardly expect success with 0.1 per cent. of the votes. But, to show that these demands are fairly modest, they outline their " historical claims," and show a big enclave which would still remain German. Unfortunately, such propaganda is carried out with great skill, and those with little knowledge of history are easily persuaded that one-third of Europe was once Polish. By no means all Poles support this propaganda, but a strong section is actively engaged in trying to make the impression that only a small part of " real Poland " was made independent by the Treaty of Versailles. Actually, much of what is now Poland has more than 50 per cent. non-Poles (see Appendix tables, based on other Polish sources).

Appendix

Table I

The following table shows that imports passing through Danzig had almost equalled those via Gdynia by 1938. They refer to tonnage only, however. Mass goods, of low value, were mainly reserved for Danzig, while valuable imports arrived through Gdynia (*See* Table III, from which it will be noticed that Danzig's share in value was a mere fraction of Gdynia's).

Year	Tonnage via Danzig	Tonnage via Gdynia
1934	655,763	991,544
1935	778,532	1,111,844
1936	953,154	1,335,456
1937	1,515,822	1,718,004
1938	1,547,866	1,526,536

Table II

Exports passing through Danzig and Gdynia were still more unfavourable for the former. Gdynia had easily outstripped Danzig. A comparison with Table IV shows that Danzig was in a much worse position as regards the value of the goods concerned.

Year	Tonnage via Danzig	Tonnage via Gdynia
1934	5,713,181	6,200,369
1935	4,324,246	6,362,599
1936	4,675,002	6,407,490
1937	5,684,849	7,288,173
1938	5,583,886	7,646,902

Table III

The percentage of imports in 1938 according to value:

Via Gdynia	Via Danzig	Otherwise imported
53·7%	7·8%	38·5%

APPENDIX

Table IV

The percentage of exports in 1938 according to value:

Via Gdynia	Via Danzig	Otherwise exported
40·6%	23·5%	35·9%

Table V

The number of ships entering and leaving Gdynia:

Year	Ships entering	Ships leaving
1924	29	29
1926	312	316
1928	1,108	1,093
1930	2,238	2,219
1932	3,610	3,604

Table VI

The percentage of foreign trade passing through Gdynia developed during the early years of the port's growth as follows:

Year	Turnover	Total via Gdynia
1929	26,125,000	10%
1930	22,493,000	14½%
1931	21,664,000	24%
1932	15,290,000	34%
1933	15,343,000	37%

APPENDIX

TABLE VII

The number of educational establishments giving instruction in the various languages spoken in the Composite State of Poland was as follows in 1929, i.e. before the action taken against the Ukrainian and other minorities:

Language	Kindergarten	Elementary	Secondary	Academic
Polish	1,588	21,806	759	22
Ukrainian	47	790	20	none
White Russian	none	26	3	none
German	34	768	29	none
Yiddish	42	177	3	none
Hebrew	35	183	11	none
Lithuanian	none	105	2	none
Polish, plus a second language	16	2,647	10	none

TABLE VIII

The teachers' training colleges in 1930 (before the anti-minority action) were as follows:

Language	No. of Training Colleges	Persons attending
Polish	198	31,300
Ukrainian	10	1,500
White Russian	none	none
German	3	400
Yiddish	1	100
Hebrew	3	300
Lithuanian	none	none

APPENDIX

TABLE IX

The percentage of various nationalities living in Poland (August, 1939):

Poles	60·16%
Ukrainians	20·06%
Jews	9·18%
White Russians	5·75%
Germans	4·22%
Lithuanians	0·57%
Others	0·07%

TABLE X

According to "Poland Old and New" (Arct, Warsaw, 1938), the proportion of Ukrainians among the indigenous population in the following districts was:

In Stanislawow	In Volhynia	In Tarnopol
70%	70%	46%

In the voivodship of Lemberg	in the voivodship of Polesia
36%	33%

TABLE XI

The population of the voivodships largely Ukrainian was at the census of December, 1935:

Stanislawow	Volhynia	Tarnopol	Lemberg	Polesia
1,477,000	2,085,000	1,603,000	3,128,000	1,131,000

APPENDIX

Important dates in Polish history:

1025. King Boleslas crowned; non-Polish area on the Baltic coast and in the North-West of his realm conquered by Boleslas.

1109. The land of the Pomeranians annexed by Poland.

1138. Following dynastic disputes, Poland split up into numerous minor States, each under its own ruler.

1226. Teutonic Knights settle in Pomerania.

1308. Danzig and Pomerania join the Teutonic Knights.

1340. The area surrounding Lemberg annexed by Poland.

1350. Great influx of Jews begins.

1370. Louis of Hungary ascended the throne of Poland.

1386. Lithuania added to Poland by peaceful measures.

1410. Teutonic Knights attacked and defeated at Grunwald.

1464. Poland annexes Pomerania. (Danzig remained more or less independent, although nominally under the Poles.)

1506. Polish expansion begins.

1525. East Prussia temporarily under Polish sovereignty.

1561. Esthonia annexed by the Poles.

1595. Polish capital moved from Cracow to Warsaw.

1648. Cossacks rebel against oppression of the Poles.

1655. Following several wars, Poles subdued by the Swedes.

1696. A Saxon king begins new Polish dynasty; Russians take action to safeguard their large minorities under Polish rule.

APPENDIX

1768. War with Russia.

1772. First partition of Poland, most of the territory going to Russia.

1793. Second partition of Poland.

1795. Third partition of Poland, Russia again taking most of the land.

1797. Polish legion joins Napoleon.

1806. Duchy of Warsaw created by Napoleon.

1815. The Congress of Vienna confirms partition of Poland. England and France especially in favour of the partition.

1830. Polish rebellion against the Russians.

1864. New rebellions of the Poles put down.

1905. Poles revolt under Pilsudski against Russians.

1908. A riflemen's corps founded by Pilsudski in Austria.

1914–1917. Poles join the Central Powers against Russia.

1916. Germans promise Poles independence.

1918. Pilsudski released at Magdeburg and elected Chief of State.

1919. Poles oppose Allies and invade Upper Silesia.

1919. Poles invade Vilna.

1920. After attacking Russia, Poles succeed in beating off the punitive army.

1921. Large part of Upper Silesia annexed.

1923. Vilna annexed.

1924. Building of Gdynia begun.

1926. Pilsudski assumes supreme control of State.

APPENDIX

1930. Pacification of the Ukrainians. Numerous villages destroyed, peasants ill-treated. Subsequent elections show a marked reduction in the Ukrainian vote.

1932. Pact of Non-Aggression with Russia.

1934. Pact of Non-Aggression with Germany. Pilsudski and Hitler arrange for a peaceful settlement of differences.

1935. Death of Marshal Pilsudski.

1936. Rydz appointed Marshal of Poland.

1937. Tension with Baltic States.

1939. Hitler's proposal for Danzig to rejoin the Reich and to build an ex-territorial road from the Reich to East Prussia rejected. German-Polish Agreement cancelled by Germany, the latter claiming that Warsaw had broken terms by agreements with third Powers. Action against German minorities. Financial difficulties owing to mobilisation.

For more books on this subject and many other little-known aspects of German history, please visit us at VersandbuchhandelScriptorium.com
and our sister site wintersonnenwende.com !

Featured publications include:

• *The Polish Atrocities Against the German Minority in Poland*. Edited and published by order of the Foreign Office and based upon documentary evidence. Volk und Reich Verlag, Berlin 1940,
as well as the German original:
• *Die polnischen Greueltaten an den Volksdeutschen in Polen*. Im Auftrage des Auswärtigen Amtes auf Grund urkundlichen Beweismaterials zusammengestellt. Volk und Reich Verlag, Berlin 1940.

• Edwin Erich Dwinger: *Death in Poland. The Fate of the Ethnic Germans in September 1939*. Scriptorium, Canada 2021.
as well as the German original:
• *Der Tod in Polen. Die volksdeutsche Passion*. Eugen Diederichs Verlag, Jena, 1940.

• Erhard Wittek: *Long Night's Journey Into Day. The Death March of Lowicz*. Scriptorium, Canada 2015.
as well as the German original:
• *Der Marsch nach Lowitsch*. Zentralverlag der NSDAP., Franz Eher Nachf. G.m.b.H., Berlin 1940.

More titles are being added regularly in German and English.

www.ingramcontent.com/pod-product-compliance
Lightning Source LLC
Chambersburg PA
CBHW050252120526
44590CB00016B/2325